CRITICAL EMPLOYMENT ISSUES FACING THE SOUTHEAST

Edited by
Bruce E. Kaufman
Department of Economics

William T. Rutherford
Department of Management

Research Monograph No. 98
1986

Business Publishing Division
College of Business Administration
Georgia State University
Atlanta, Georgia

Library of Congress Cataloging-in-Publication Data

Main entry under title:

Critical employment issues facing the Southeast

(Research monograph/College of Business Administration, Georgia State University ; 98.)
Papers originally presented at a conference held at Georgia State University, February 22, 1983.
Includes bibliographical references.
1. Employment forecasting—Southern States—Congresses. 2. Foreign trade and employment—Southern States—Congresses. I. Kaufman, Bruce E. II. Rutherford, William T. III. Georgia State University. College of Business Administration. IV. Series: Research monograph (Georgia State University. College of Business Administration) ; no. 98.
HD5725.S85C75   1986   331.12′5′0975   85-31410
ISBN 0-88406-191-4

Published by:
Business Publishing Division
College of Business Administration
Georgia State University
University Plaza
Atlanta, Georgia 30303-3093
Telephone: 404/658-4253

Cover design by Marcia L. Lampe.

This volume is dedicated to William T. Rutherford who died on October 14, 1984. He was an outstanding teacher and scholar, and a warm-hearted human being.

Contents

Dr. William T. Rutherford Remembered

One wonders what features of an all too short professional life ought to be highlighted here. The effort is particularly challenging where the individual's interest, activity, and excellence was so widespread and diverse. Yet such was the nature of the man, William T. Rutherford. In his fourteen-year academic career at Georgia State University, Bill truly and uniquely distinguished himself as teacher, as researcher, in institutional service, and in the community at large.

Bill brought a rather rare yet terribly appropriate background to the university in the fall of 1970. He had a solid grounding in the workings of the U.S. economic system and the labor market by virtue of two degrees in economics earned at the University of Tennessee. A law degree from the University of Michigan sharpened his analytic skills and helped provide the logical approach to problem identification and solution for which he became known. His years with the National Labor Relations Board directed his interest to the field of labor relations, a natural outgrowth of training in economics and the law, and also gave him that insight into the attitudes and perspectives of everyday workers that was the hallmark of his approach to all subsequent work.

Dr. Rutherford's engaging personality and unique perceptions captivated audiences as dissimilar as middle- and upper-level executives in a management development program and shop stewards in a labor relations training institute. His insightful yet always fair-minded and disinterested presentations challenged each group to explore all sides of an issue in labor law, collective bargaining, or labor arbitration—never knowing for sure until the close of the discussion what stance he ultimately would take on the matter at hand.

Bill was a strong believer in the biblical precept, "Come let us reason together." He played a vital role in the early 1970s in rejuvenating an inactive local chapter of the Industrial Relations Research Association and remained active as officer and participant thereafter. As the principal organization designed to bring together practitioners from all facets of the labor and industrial relations field, it was altogether fitting and proper that Dr. Rutherford would view it as a natural activity to pursue—and pursue it he did, with characteristic success. Within the university, Bill was elected to the university senate the first year it was established. This further testimony to the esteem in which he was held also reflected his desire to be an active participant in deliberative, forward-looking, decision-making bodies that encompassed diverse views and perspectives.

Dr. Rutherford was a gifted, extensively accepted, and widely used labor arbitrator. By personality and background he was especially equipped to serve in this quasi-judicial capacity, and he carried it off splendidly for more than ten years. Attorneys from both sides of the table, union business agents, and corporate personnel directors all uniformly sang his praises. But equally important to Bill was always the fact that the supervisor and the grievant also could relate to him, his conduct of the hearing, and his written award. In an age where arbitral decisions have seemed to take on more and more the legal jargon and trappings of the increasingly legalistic employment relationship, he retained the capacity to write decisions that the diverse readership could understand and, typically, accept. One could not help but be aware of the variety of people who had come into contact with him in the labor relations arena who then were impressed with his capacity to be fair, just, and extremely likable. Yet he was more than that as a labor arbitrator. Asked at arbitration training programs to identify the most critical characteristic of a good arbitrator, Bill always unhesitatingly responded, "To be courageous." A perusal of his arbitration decisions quickly reveals that he succeeded admirably.

Notwithstanding these diverse achievements, Bill was first and foremost an outstanding teacher, and it was his role as professor he most cherished. His class sessions were spirited and challenging, and students loved to hear him relate prior cases in which he had been involved at the NLRB or as an arbitrator. He had the knack of entertaining while informing, always calling forth the best his students could deliver. Praise from students for a job well done was always the praise he most cherished.

The conference that produced the distinguished papers presented in this volume was Dr. Rutherford's last major professional undertaking. He found his interaction on this project with Dr. Bruce Kaufman to be enriching, and he was rightfully pleased with the caliber of papers that resulted. A most fitting statement was offered Bill in the last performance appraisal he received from his then department chairman and now dean of the College of Business Administration, Dr. Michael H. Mescon. It said, in relevant part:

> Bill, you've been a powerful role model and source of inspiration to all of your colleagues. Although I have just the faintest inkling of what you've faced and are presently confronting, I do know that you have not neglected your institutional responsibilities.
>
> I particularly applaud your continued excellence in the classroom and your many contributions in the continuing education arena. Also, the work with Dr. Kaufman should result in a significant publication. I know you've been working on this for quite a while, and I look forward to its publication.

Now its publication is at hand. Bill would have liked it. It is typical of everything he did—first class!

Dr. Michael Jay Jedel
Director
Institute of Industrial Relations
Georgia State University

Preface

The papers in this volume were prepared for a conference on "Critical Employment Issues Facing the Southeast in the 1980s" held at Georgia State University on February 22, 1983. The purpose of the conference was to provide a forum in which a broad range of employment issues confronting the states of the southeast region could be discussed and debated by recognized experts in the field. In discussing these employment issues, we instructed our authors to not only examine past trends but, more importantly, to look ahead through the rest of the decade and identify what they foresaw as the critical problems or developments that would confront workers, business firms, and policymakers. We hoped that this long-range view of employment issues in the Southeast would prove useful in focusing public attention on areas of concern that may be only dimly perceived now but will be of growing importance in the years ahead.

In organizing the conference, we deliberately included topics that covered a wide range of issues associated with employment. We also chose our authors for the variety of viewpoints and backgrounds they could bring to the subject. Finally, we instructed our authors to focus on the states in the southeastern United States as much as possible. We did this partly because the region is, in many ways, unique in its political and economic heritage, and partly because this allowed our authors to take a more in-depth look at issues or problems specific to these states that no other study has addressed.

To introduce the subject of critical employment issues in the Southeast, we chose the foremost expert in the field, F. Ray Marshall. Marshall's paper provides an overview of the unique economic and political heritage of the states of the Southeast. He then discusses in some detail a wide range of employment issues that are likely to affect the region—issues such as the threat of foreign competition to the region's dominant industries, the implications of federal government expenditure and taxation policies for regional employment, and the labor market effects of illegal immigration.

Our next two authors, Donald Ratajczak and Ronald Robinson, take a much more detailed look at future trends in employment, income, and economic growth in the Southeast. One of their major conclusions is that the rate of employment growth in the Southeast in the 1980s will probably lag behind the rapid growth in jobs experienced in the 1970s. Compared to other regions of the nation, however, the states of the Southeast will probably continue to enjoy greater rates of capital investment and job creation in the 1980s. They also show that the pattern of economic growth in the 1980s will be very uneven among different states and demographic groups in the region.

The next set of papers by Gretchen Maclachlan and David Moore focuses on human resource and personal issues facing the states of the Southeast. Maclachlan examines the disparities between white and minority workers in the region's work force with respect to key labor market outcomes such as unemployment, per capita income, the incidence of poverty, and labor force participation. She foresees only a limited narrowing in the historic differentials that have separated the two groups of workers. Moore analyzes the major developments in the field of personnel that are likely to affect business firms in the Southeast. Among the critical employment issues he identifies is the need for a more participative style of management and the importance of improved productivity through the removal of archaic or restrictive work practices.

The final two papers by Bruce Raynor and Curtis Mack focus on the outlook for labor relations in the Southeast for the remainder of the 1980s. Raynor argues that many employment problems such as raising productivity or meeting the threat of foreign competition require a cooperative effort between employers and unions. In his view, however, as long as employers in the region continue to attack the organizational security of the unions, conflict—not cooperation—will be the major theme in labor relations. Mack takes a different perspective, focusing on the instability imparted to labor relations in the region by the growing politicization of the National Labor Relations Board.

We hope these papers provide the reader with considerable insight and information on economic and social conditions in the states of the Southeast. Our chief desire, however, is that the attempt of our authors to peer into the future will help spark greater awareness and discussion on the part of concerned citizens and policymakers concerning critical employment issues that face the region in the remainder of the 1980s.

CHAPTER ONE

Key Labor Problems
in the Southeast in the 1980s

F. RAY MARSHALL

Professor of Economics, University of Texas–Austin
U.S. Secretary of Labor, 1977–1981

Introduction

The key labor problems of the Southeast during the 1980s will be similar to those of the rest of the United States but will differ in nature and intensity. Of course, the definition of labor problems depends on the perspective taken. From the employers' perspective, the key problem will be to obtain qualified workers at a competitive wage. "Qualified" will increasingly mean workers with a good basic education and technical and quantitative skills. A major problem is likely to be a shortage of skilled professional and technical workers, who now often must be imported from other regions. Employers will also need to incorporate workers into *management systems* that will make their companies competitive with respect to productivity and quality in an increasingly internationalized market. Traditional authoritative American management styles (along with noncompetitive prices and quality) are being challenged by participative systems (developed by some

1

foreign and American companies) that appear to be more productive than the traditional American hierarchical system.

For low-income workers in the South—especially blacks and other minorities—a major problem of the 1980s will be *unemployment* and *low wages*. Low-income people—especially blacks in lagging rural places—did not benefit as much as whites from economic growth during the 1950s and 1960s and are likely to be the chief losers from high levels of unemployment and slow growth during the 1980s, the weakening of federal human resource development and income support programs, and the adverse effects of Reaganomics. Low- and middle-income people are likely to pay a relatively larger share of taxes during the 1980s than they have in the past, mainly because of the regressivity of both the 1981 tax cuts and higher state and local taxes levied to compensate for cuts in federal programs. Workers at the low end of the wage scale are likely to suffer disproportionately from intensified international trade competition because many of the marginal low-wage jobs in the Southeast are on their way to the Third World. Low-wage workers will, in addition, be the principal losers because of immigration from Third World countries, countries that are likely to have very high levels of unemployment and underemployment for the rest of this century.

Southern workers also will have a problem protecting themselves from arbitrary management decisions in an increasingly competitive economic environment. Enlightened managers will attempt to treat their workers with dignity and will encourage worker participation in production decisions to promote worker identification with their companies, thereby increasing productivity and improving the quality of output. But competition often causes employers to shift the costs of change to workers. Southern workers are not as well organized as workers outside the South and therefore have less ability to protect themselves from arbitrary decisions or from unsafe or unhealthy work environments. However, low-income southern workers are likely to compensate for their collective bargaining weaknesses with greater political action in order to substitute government protections for bargaining weaknesses; the political competition resulting from the erosion of the South's traditional one-party system and the Civil Rights Act of 1964 have increased the political power of low-income southerners.

From the public's perspective, the South's leaders must develop policies and programs that create an environment in which economic development (not just growth) can continue, mediate conflicting labor market interests, and provide quality education and training. This will allow workers to improve their skills, especially in the growing high-tech occupations that, for a time at least, are likely to be competitive in international markets. Continued improvement in the quality of industry in the South will require careful attention to selectivity in the kinds of industry sought and the development of human resources. Southern political leaders must also pursue development strategies that allow economic adjustment, as some industries shrink or evaporate and others expand. Measures must likewise be developed to improve the operation of labor markets—especially better labor market information systems and mechanisms to facilitate the adjustment of workers from declining industries to growth occupations and industries. Public policy should ensure a more equitable sharing of the benefits and costs of change.

In order to promote the effective development of all of the South's people, public authorities must promote more equal access to education, training, and jobs, and reduce discrimination against women, minorities, and older workers. The rapid increase in the labor force participation of women will cause pay equity and affirmative action to be important issues during the 1980s.

A major problem for southern governments will be the need to adjust to an environment of slower growth in productivity and total output, intensified international competition, monetary policies based on a fear of reigniting inflation, and federal policies much less favorable to the South than those that prevailed from the 1930s to 1981. The South is likely to lose, relative to other regions, from Reaganomics, the New Federalism, and increased military spending.

Let me now examine these issues in greater detail by tracing the main trends in the South and their implications for workers.

The South in Transition

The South has entered what some call the Sunbelt phase, as distinguished from the Traditional South of the 1890s when the South's basic social and economic institutions were differentiated from those of the rest of the United States and from the New or Industrializing South, which saw the South's institutions and socioeconomic indicators converging with those of the rest of the country, after having diverged since early in the nineteenth century. Because of the region's rapid growth during the 1960s and 1970s, some people believe the South will pull ahead of the rest of the country during the Sunbelt phase.

My main purpose is to discuss these trends and their implications for workers, employers, and public policy.

The Transitions

The Traditional South, which became established roughly between 1890 and 1910, could be defined statistically as: agrarian, especially plantation agriculture; racially segregated; having a one-party political tradition; Protestant; native-born; and having lower incomes and education, among other characteristics.

The New South was characterized by industrialization, especially the growth of manufacturing, that eroded the region's traditional institutions and created a slow convergence of most statistical indicators with the non-South, since the rates of growth in the South have been faster than the rest of the country.[1] The South's industrial mix shifted away from agriculture to more diversified nonfarm activities; the region's economic elites became more pluralistic; the Republican party became stronger; and legal segregation was eliminated and blacks were drawn more into the mainstream of political and social life. Per capita income regained 1860 levels relative to the entire United States in 1920 in the Southwest (72 percent), between 1940-1950 in the South Atlantic (65 percent), and between 1960-65 in the East South Central (68 percent).

In 1980 per capita income ranged from about 71 percent of the national average in Mississippi to 99 percent in Texas. Virginia, Florida, and metropolitan parts of other states probably have *real* incomes equal to the national average. However, we do not have adequate measures of geographical cost of living differentials to make this judgment with much confidence.

Basic Trends

Initially industrialization in the South was heavily concentrated in marginal, low-wage *manufacturing* (especially textiles and food processing), which is still more important in the South than in the non-South; but the trend is toward *services*, especially the information occupations. In the United States, information occupations (according to some definitions) were 17 percent of the work force in 1950 and are 60 percent today. This trend, which is one of the most important in the South, the United States, and the world, has had the following effects:

1. Local newspaper information monopolies were broken with the advent of electronic media.

2. During the 1970s, nonmetropolitan areas in the United States gained 880,000 nonfarm jobs, while metropolitan areas lost 217,000 nonfarm jobs. This decentralization was facilitated by improved communications and other information technology.

3. Smaller work forces—60 percent of the job growth during the 1970s is estimated to have been in plants with twenty or fewer workers; 70 percent of the growth in the South is estimated to have been in plants with less than fifty employees. The new information systems have also helped to reduce plant size.

The information revolution will continue to have a profound impact on the United States, the world, and the Southeast. It will change the kinds of jobs people have, the size of the work places, where people work, how they live and play, and how they learn. In fact, the significance of the information revolution is so pervasive as to be only dimly and imperfectly predictable.

A major concern for the South must be to see to it that education and training systems do not widen the employment opportunity gaps between higher-income people, who have the technical education to benefit from the high-tech occupations, and lower-income people and minorities, who have much lower levels of technical and scientific education.

The *internationalization* of the American economy has contributed to the economic development of the South. A large percentage of the output of southern farms and factories enters international trade, which accounted for about 9 percent of U.S. gross national product in 1950 and almost 25 percent by 1981. Moreover, intensified international competition has contributed to the relative decline of the industrial Northeast and Midwest and the growth of industry seeking low labor costs and other lower costs in the South. Increasing global interdependence also means that Sunbelt industry must compete in international trade. For some labor-intensive activities, wages in the South are not likely to continue to be competitive with the Third World, and competition from industrialized countries like Japan will probably continue to be intense, although the Japanese probably will slow down during the 1980s. Competition from other newly industrializing and lesser developed countries will intensify, however. International competition is stimulated by multinational corporations whose global strategies are greatly strengthened by new information systems. Wage differentials are too great, and these countries have governmental, organizational, and human resource advantages, which are causing U.S. companies (and could cause the South) to lose competitive position.

According to the International Labor Organization (ILO), Third World countries will have to generate 600 to 700 million jobs by the year 2000 just to keep unemployment and underemployment from rising above 40 or 50 percent. To put this in perspective, there are not 600 million jobs in the industrialized market economies today. These Third World workers will impact the South through trade and immigration.

The displacement of southern agriculture has had several significant effects:

1. Approximately 2.3 million full-time equivalent jobs were eliminated from southern agriculture between 1950 and 1970.[2]

2. Most of these displaced workers were not prepared for urban or nonfarm jobs.

3. The movement out of low-productivity agriculture into higher-productivity urban occupations contributed to increased national

productivity but created problems for urban areas to which these workers migrated, as well as for the depopulated areas of the rural South from which they moved.

The racial patterns of the movement out of southern agriculture were different. Southern whites were more likely to move to small towns and cities in the South, while blacks were more likely to move to larger metropolitan areas where other blacks were concentrated.
The evidence suggests that black migrants from the rural South often had less unemployment in northern labor markets than blacks with similar characteristics who were born there. This labor market phenomenon is similar to that observed with migrants from Third World countries: recent migrants with Third World aspirations are more willing to take low-status jobs; thus they are preferred by employers for low-wage, marginal jobs. As time passes, however, the migrants acquire the job attitudes and aspirations that prevail in the places to which they have moved. Employers then seek new sources of labor for low-status jobs as alternatives to mechanization, higher wages, or the migration of physical facilities. With the virtual exhaustion of net outmigration from the rural South in the 1960s, employers turned increasingly to legal and illegal immigrants as a new source of labor for marginal, low-wage jobs.

Controversy exists regarding the impact of immigration on domestic workers. Some argue that the immigrants only fill jobs that domestic workers will not take and therefore do not contribute to unemployment. My own view is that while the immigrants do not displace domestic workers on a one-for-one basis, they *do* displace *some* workers and contribute to the perpetuation of low-wage, marginal jobs. Illegal immigration perpetuates an underclass of easily exploited workers who have limited power to complain about exploitation. The displacement is not one-for-one because some of the jobs would otherwise (a) go to the Third World; (b) be mechanized; (c) pay higher wages; or (d) disappear altogether. Doubtless, illegal immigration depresses wages and working conditions, especially during times of unemployment. It could be argued that during periods of relatively full employment, immigrants fill low-wage jobs that otherwise could not be filled at going wages from the domestic work force, thus accelerating economic growth and the upward mobility of domestic workers. However, this is mainly a short-run phenomenon with important long-run social, political, and economic consequences, as the West Europeans are discovering from their guest-worker experience. Theories that treat labor as a commodity often create serious social problems. As one European writer put it, "We asked for labor and got people."

4. The movement of people out of the rural South also set in motion important national and international political forces—especially the civil rights movement—which in turn had a profound impact on the South and the nation.

During the 1960s and 1970s, migration into the South and backmigration of southerners contributed to and reflected the convergence of per capita incomes between the South and non-South.

It is necessary to be cautious about exaggerating the decline of the Northeast and Midwest:

1. Concentration on trends and percentages can distort conclusions.

2. In relative terms, six of the ten slowest-growing states (New York, Illinois, Ohio, Michigan, Pennsylvania, and New Jersey) probably will have the largest absolute gains by the year 2000.[3]

3. The states with the slowest growth will gain about $69 billion more (1972 dollars) in absolute terms by 2000 than the ten fastest-growing states.

4. Between 1978 and 2000, per capita incomes in the Sunbelt (Southwest, Rocky Mountains, Southeast, and Far West) will shift from 97 percent of the national average to 98 percent—one point over twenty-two years. Per capita incomes in the Southeast will shift from 87 percent to 93 percent of the national average, but only Virginia and Texas are expected to equal the national average by 2000.

Consequences of Transition

With improved *incomes* and the convergence of *political*, *economic*, and *social institutions* with those of the rest of the

United States, the South has been drawn increasingly into the United States (New South) and the world (Sunbelt) economies.

Political and Social Consequence

As noted, industrialization eroded the South's traditional racial and political institutions and introduced political pluralism, leading to the breakup of the one-party system. However, developments since World War II also have weakened the traditional Democratic party coalition—southern blacks still vote Democratic, but whites have switched to the Republican party in national elections. They apparently believe they no longer need the government and have reacted negatively to civil rights and Great Society programs.

The nation therefore has political instability because of unstable *ad hoc* political majorities: Populist, 24 percent (liberal economics, conservative culture); Liberal, 16 percent (liberal economics and culture); Conservative, 16 percent (conservative economics and culture); and Libertarian, 13 percent (conservative economics, liberal culture).

The Growth of Unions

The South has a long tradition of workers' organizations. Early working men's associations were formed in the eighteenth century. Craft unions were organized in the early nineteenth century. The earliest collective bargaining union I know about is the New Orleans Typographical Union, formed in 1810. Many of the early leaders of the International Typographical Union, the oldest union, were from the South, and several other unions, most notably the International Association of Machinists, were formed in the South.[4]

Some of the main conclusions about unions in the South are:

1 Labor movements are inevitable products of industrialization. The choice has not been whether labor organizations emerge, but what kind of labor organizations prevail.

2. Except for the crafts, unions were incompatible with traditional agrarian southern institutions controlled mainly by economic elites, which were at first agrarian and then agrarian and business combinations allied with "white supremacy" political

forces. Until the post-World War II period, and after the Populist experience, workers were segregated.

3. Unions in the South have matched the growth of unions in the United States. They peaked during World War II but have since declined *relative to the work force*. But this is a deceptive measure because (a) it includes employers, professionals, and others; and (b) unions and employee associations are only about 27 percent of the work force, but collective bargaining covers perhaps 45 percent to 50 percent of nonfarm wages, and has a strong impact on the rest.

It is also important to recognize that union membership increased from 15 million in 1948 to 24 million in 1980, an increase of 60 percent. The South is only about half as well organized as the rest of the country (14 percent and 29 percent in 1978), but union membership has grown much faster in the South than in the non-South (37 percent for the South and only 4.6 percent for the non-South from 1966-1976). Absolute membership increased from 2,168,000 in 1966 to 2,970,000 in 1976. In 1978, southern unions and associations had 3,746,000 members. Nevertheless, unions are losing their relative strength in some industries (construction, coal mining) and are not keeping pace with the growth of the work force.

However, these generalizations about unions mask considerable diversity. In a few places and industries, unions are better organized in the South than they are elsewhere. For example, the aircraft, chemical, petroleum, and paper products industries were as well or better organized in the South than elsewhere.[5] However, important southern industries like food processing and construction are much less organized in the South than in other parts of the United States (20 percent and 44 percent to 22 percent and 49 percent, respectively).

Unions are generally weaker in the South because:

1. The South has relatively more poorly organized, marginal, labor-intensive, low-wage, highly competitive industry. Moreover, the composition of southern employment is shifting more to women and to professional-technical and white-collar jobs.

2. The nonmetropolitan location of most southern manufacturing plant employment is increasingly in *smaller* plants. Unions have been stronger in large urban plants.

3. Community opposition has regarded unions as impediments to growth and productivity. Unions also challenge traditional political power structures. A major reason for the prevalence of "right to work" laws in the South is to advertise antiunion sentiments in an effort to attract industry.

4. Some industries—construction, coal mining, manufacturing— that in the past have formed the hard core of the unions' strength are declining.

5. Employer opposition, aided by relatively weak penalties for labor law violations, is increasing and has become more sophisticated.

The outlook of the unions depends on what happens in the country. I expect unions to continue to grow and to be an important political and economic force but to lose their relative strength in industries like construction and durable goods manufacturing in the short run.

Unions will grow in public employment and among white-collar workers. As has always been the case, there will be spurts in membership during special times of ferment such as in 1937 and during World War II.

However, none of this is predetermined. With effective internal union structure and leadership and more positive public opinion and effective public policies, the ability of workers to organize would be strengthened. Under present arrangements, the penalties for violating the National Labor Relations Act (NLRA) are too weak to be a deterrent to determined violators. I therefore expect unions to become more active politically in an effort to compensate for economic weaknesses.

Poverty and Low Wages

It would be a mistake to leave the impression that the convergence of incomes between the South and the rest of the country eliminated the problems of poverty and low wages. This is not the case because the South's industrialization has not benefited all people and areas equally.

Some People Left Out of the Transition

Poverty: One-sixth of the South and one-eleventh of the non-South, including 15 percent of southern nonmetropolitan whites and 44 percent of nonmetropolitan blacks, were below the poverty line in 1980. In metropolitan areas, 8.9 percent of southern whites and 30.8 percent of blacks were poor in 1980. There are more poor whites, but the incidence of poverty is much higher in rural areas and among blacks. The southern poor also are more likely to be the working poor.

Industrialization has bypassed rural counties with heavy black populations. In those 244 counties with 5,000-plus blacks, conditions in 1960 were improved by industrialization, but poverty is still much greater for blacks than for whites.[6] From 1960 to 1970, poverty in these counties declined from 81 percent to 56 percent for blacks, and 32 percent to 20 percent for whites. Blacks lost 97,000 jobs in these counties, while whites gained 287,000. Manufacturing also has tended to avoid rural areas dominated by agribusiness and areas where unions were strong, as well as places with heavy black populations.

Wages: Despite the convergence of incomes, wages in the South generally lag behind those of other regions because of the more unequal distribution of income. Moreover, North-South wage differentials remained surprisingly stable at about 17 percent between 1973 and 1978.

Of the main determinants of these wage differentials, unions and collective bargaining are one of the most important. The wages of unionized workers are 22 percent above those of nonunion workers with similar characteristics.[7]

But much of the South's employment is heavily concentrated in industries that are not well organized. Wages in the South were less than 80 percent of those in the non-South between 1973 and 1978. Within the South, nonunion manufacturing workers earned only 75 percent as much as their union counterparts. Within the same industry (or Standard Industrial Classification), the South/non-South differential was 95 percent for unionized workers and 90 percent for nonunion workers. Other South/non-South differentials in 1978 included:

Type of Work	Percentage of Non-South Wages
White collar	92%
Blue collar	78
Service	89

Differentials also vary by education:

Education in Years	Percentage of Non-South Wages
1–8	78%
9–11	91
12	86
16	92
17	93

Differentials also vary by age, suggesting "vintage" of education and training. Thus 16- to 24-year-olds earn 93 percent of non-South wages, while 55- to 64-year-olds earn only 78 percent of non-South wages.

The differentials also vary by race. Blacks earn 82 percent of whites in the United States but blacks in the South earn 78 percent of whites; blacks in the non-South earn 99 percent of whites; and blacks in the South earn only 68 percent of blacks in the non-South.

The gross wage differential between the South and the rest of the country was 11 percentage points, according to a 1981 Bureau of Labor Statistics study.[8] Regression analysis identified some of the major causes of this wage gap as due to differences in the percent of the work force unionized (three points); the proportion of nonwhites in the work force (two points); productivity differences among workers (two points); city size (two points); and the sex composition of the work force (zero points).

A number of forces suggest that economic development of the South will not be as rapid during the rest of this century as it has been during the past twenty years:

1. The Deep South has become more vulnerable to economic

slumps. In 1982, five Deep South states had double-digit levels of unemployment when the national unemployment rate was 8.9 percent (Alabama, Arkansas, Mississippi, South Carolina, and Tennessee).

2. Costs of production and consumer prices are increasing faster in the South than elsewhere, according to a statement by Bernard Weinstein to the southern Governors' Conference in the fall of 1981.

3. Though wage differentials are not converging as rapidly as incomes (because income differentials are greater in the South), they are slowly narrowing, and this trend will reduce the South's attractiveness to low-wage industry. However, the continuation of illegal immigration, the fact that the South has a net immigration of low-wage workers, the higher levels of unemployment in the South, and the anticipated generally depressed conditions of low-wage marginal industries will be important factors.

Moreover, wage differentials are offset somewhat by lower levels of education, training, and productivity in the South. For example, a 1981 article by Edward Miller concluded that although a few industries have higher productivity in the South than elsewhere, "wages in the South are about 8 percent lower than they are in the rest of the nation, but the output for each worker hour is typically 4 percent lower."[9] However, profits remain higher in the South because wages have lagged considerably farther behind productivity than they have in the rest of the country.[10]

4. The Reagan administration's policies will hurt the South because those policies are very regressive (as well as economically repressive), and the South has heavy concentrations of poor people—especially the working poor—who are the main losers from the administration's tax and budget policies.[11]

While there is some logic in shifting program responsibility to state and local areas, there are also major problems:

(a) Funds are being cut, and the states are not taking up the slack. Under the administration's plans, federal aid will decline from about 25 percent of state and local budgets in 1980 to 3 to 4 percent by 1991.

(b) Even the slack taken up results in regressive taxes, which hurt low-income people and make the South's income differentials even more unequal.

(c) No constituents exist in many state and local areas for human resource development programs for the disadvantaged.

(d) There is a danger of devaluation of human resource development programs as states compete for industry.

(e) The administration's welfare programs on the average place a 95 percent tax on the earnings of Aid for Dependent Children recipients, who are not likely to improve their positions very much even in a growing economy—which itself is not likely for the foreseeable future.

(f) As a poor region, the South has benefited disproportionately from federal expenditures and will therefore lose disproportionately from the reduction of these expenditures since 1981. For example, per capita federal taxes in the East South Central states in 1980 were $1,767, and federal expenditures were $2,272.

(g) The South will benefit less than other regions from the planned defense build-up: an increase of 37 percent for the Pacific states by 1986, 16 percent for New England, 14 percent for the East North Central, but only 5.7 percent for the East South Central and 4.3 percent for the West South Central.[12]

The net income flows per capita resulting from the administration's tax and spending policies by 1986 include: Pacific, $1,408 (the highest); West South Central, $1,071; and East South Central, $611 (the lowest).

The Reagan administration's policies also will hurt the South by withdrawing federal infrastructure and human resource development that the South has not been able to generate for itself. Because the South has been the poorest region, it has been particularly dependent on federal aid. Programs that have been especially helpful to the South include mass transportation, job training, and funds for water and sewer improvements.[13]

5. Northern states that have lost industry are stepping up their industrial development activities and can be expected to be more competitive in the future than they have been in the past. Moreover, declining growth in productivity and total output will cause non-South states to be less willing to help the South through net federal transfers. The breakup of the traditional Democratic party coalition could cause the region to have less political stability and to benefit less from powerful southern Democratic congressional leaders. However, much depends on formal political

alliances that will support policies to promote human resource development in the South and sustain more effective national and international policies.

The Outlook

The outlook for low-income and rural southerners is not very bright for the rest of this decade. However, these conditions are not predetermined and can be altered by organizational and political action to change regressive federal policies and to make state and local governments more responsive to human needs. Major efforts must be taken to get low-income people more active politically and to strengthen educational and job opportunities. Nothing would help all southerners more than full-employment policies by the federal government and greater attention to human resources development at all levels.

Summary and Conclusions

The South has gone through the transition from the Traditional to the New or Industrializing South and is currently in the Sunbelt phase. These transitions have been accompanied by the transformation of the region's traditional political, social, and economic institutions. The South's economic structure has become more diversified, its political institutions more pluralistic, and its social structure more egalitarian—especially with respect to race. There has been a slow convergence of per capita incomes between the South and the rest of the nation. Indeed, in some places—in states like Virginia and Texas, in some metropolitan areas, and for some people (more highly skilled, educated, professional, and technical workers)—real incomes could now be equal to or higher than in the non-South.

The relatively rapid growth of the South's employment and population and converging per capita incomes has resulted in a popular impression that the Sunbelt South is pulling ahead of the rest of the country. However, this is an exaggeration caused by concentrating on percentage changes rather than on absolute numbers. It is likely to be a long time before most southern states pull ahead of the rest of the United States. The center of economic gravity is shifting to the Sunbelt, but except for unusual states like Virginia, Florida, and Texas, that center is likely to remain in the industrial heartland of the North and East. Although they can be changed through policies, there are some powerful trends and forces that will cause the economic development of the South to be less rapid in the future than it has been in the past. These include:

1. A heavier concentration of marginal, low-wage industries that will be vulnerable to competition from the Third World.

2. Lower levels of education, training, and productivity in the South, which will make it more difficult to adapt to the emerging information occupations.

3. The economic drag of higher levels of poverty and underdevelopment, especially among blacks and rural people.

4. Slow growth in the national economy and in economic income support, and promotion of human resource development policies less favorable to the South than formerly.

5. Increased competition for jobs from the northern states and the erosion of some of the South's traditional advantages in attracting industry. (More supportive national policies and greater attention to the development of people could cause the southern states to overcome some of these forces and accelerate the economic improvement of southern workers.)

6. The climate for management and labor relations in the South also will be an important labor problem. The South's opposition to unions and collective bargaining probably is moderating as the South's economic structure converges with that of the non-South, reducing the desire to attract industry at any cost as a major factor in public opposition to collective bargaining.

There is some evidence—which I find convincing—that, in general, collective bargaining improves productivity.[14] This is compatible with the belief that in modern information-oriented production processes, greater worker participation in production decisions can improve quality and productivity. There also is some evidence that the adversarial relationships between labor and management and the public and private sectors have put American firms at a competitive disadvantage in improving productivity and international competitiveness. A major factor in this adversarial relationship is management resistance to the right of unions to exist, in sharp contrast to the attitudes of management in other industrial market economies. The price of union cooperation and responsibility is mutual acceptance.

The basic policy of the United States since the 1930s has been to leave the choice of collective bargaining mainly to workers, where doubts are resolved by elections supervised by the National Labor Relations Board. There was an implicit social contract during the 1930s that American unions—in contrast to their counterparts in other industrialized countries—explicitly accepted the capitalist system, and management accepted the right of workers to decide for themselves whether or not they wanted collective bargaining. There also was an acceptance of the proposition that free and democratic labor movements were essential to free and democratic societies. The rejection of this philosophy by American employers could exacerbate labor-management relations.

I believe it is in the public interest to preserve the right of workers to organize and bargain collectively and resist the philosophy that a "union-free environment" is in the public interest. While other forms of worker participation are emerging in the United States, collective bargaining will probably continue to be the main direct vehicle through which workers protect themselves on the job. Southern states could do much to promote more co-operative—and, I believe, more productive—relationships.

Endnotes

1. Philip Rones, "Moving to the Sun: Regional Job Growth 1968–1978," *Monthly Labor Review* (March 1980).

2. F. Ray Marshall and Virgil Christian, eds., *Employment of Blacks in the South* (Austin, Texas: University of Texas Press, 1978).

3. U.S. Department of Commerce, Bureau of Economic Analysis, *State Projections of Personal Income to the Year 2000*, BEA-80-84 (9 December 1980).

4. F. Ray Marshall, *Labor in the South* (Cambridge, Massachusetts: Harvard University Press, 1967).

5. George Stamas, "The Puzzling Lag in Southern Earnings," *Monthly Labor Review* (June 1981).

6. Marshall and Christian, *Employment of Blacks in the South*.

7. Stamas, "The Puzzling Lag in Southern Earnings."

8. Ibid.

9. E. Miller, "Regional Differences in Productivity, Profitability and Wages," *Texas Business Review* (May/June 1981).

10. *New York Times*, 12 March 1982.

11. F. Ray Marshall, *An Economic Strategy for the 1980's: The Failure of Reaganomics and the Full Employment Alternative* (Washington, D.C.: The National Policy Exchange and the Full Employment Action Council, 1982).

12. John Palmer and Isabel Sawhill, eds., *The Reagan Experiment* (Washington, D.C.: The Urban Institute, 1982).

13. George B. Autry, "New Federalism in the South," *Adherent* (Winter 1982).

14. F. Ray Marshall, *Industrial Relations, Worker Participation and Productivity* (New York: Economic Policy Council of the United Nations Association, 1982).

CHAPTER TWO

Labor Market Trends in the Southeast in the 1980s

DONALD RATAJCZAK
Professor of Economics and Director,
Economic Forecasting Center
Georgia State University

Introduction

Analyzing the developments in labor markets in the Southeast requires wading through several different definitions of the Southeast. In the following discussion, the Southeast sometimes will include only the eight states studied by the regional Bureau of Labor Statistics. At other times it will include the South Atlantic and East South Central states that constitute the census group. While both groups have considerable overlap, the South Atlantic area includes Maryland, Delaware, and the District of Columbia. All of these states and areas experience per capita incomes above the national average and clearly exhibit characteristics that are significantly different from southern states. The Southeast in the Bureau of Labor Statistics analysis excludes Virginia but includes the four states of the East South Central region. Failure to have a uniform definition of the Southeast is based on limitations created by the availability of regional data.

During the last decade, the Southeast exhibited greater employment and population growth and lower unemployment rates than the nation as a whole. Although female participation rates increased sharply, overall participation rates continue to be lower in most southern states than in the nation. Moreover, the participation rates grew more slowly in the Southeast than nationwide. Because male participation rates declined about as rapidly in this region as in the nation, the greater employment opportunities created a significant inflow of population. For the region as a whole, population grew about 1.6 percent per year during the last decade, almost twice as rapidly as in the nation.

Despite substantial gains in durable manufacturing, where wages converged on national levels, per capita incomes in the southern region showed little tendency to further their movement toward the national median in the last decade. For example, the regional average of personal income per capita was 84 percent of the national total in 1970 and rose to just less than 86 percent in 1980. Clearly, the slower gains in labor force participation have contributed to this slowing in the income convergence in the Southeast toward national norms.

Adjusted for compositional changes, manufacturing wages in the South remain nearly 19 percent below those in the nation. Because the workweek of southern workers is about 2 percent longer than nationally, earnings per week are about 17 percent lower than earnings nationwide. Therefore, the South remains the low-wage region of the country.

Union membership is a smaller concentration of employment in every state of the South than in the nation as a whole, although the United Mine Workers are instrumental in preserving Kentucky ratios near national norms. Surprisingly, Alabama has maintained a relatively constant percentage of its work force in unions, even as union membership as a percentage of total employment has declined in the nation. Union membership is especially low in the Carolinas and has shown little tendency to increase in importance over the last twenty years. In general, the concentration of union membership has declined more slowly in the South than nationwide, but total concentrations are only half those of the nation. Moreover, where unionization is heavily concentrated, work stoppages are relatively high. Hours lost to work stoppages are twice the national average in Alabama and Kentucky. They are below national norms in most other states of the South.

While this description of labor market conditions in the South is constructive, it only indirectly raises several important issues regarding employment in the South In the 1980s. First, a significant amount of the relative expansion in southern employment appears to be related to a filling-in of the infrastructure. Unless new basic industries are developed, the South's ability to maintain its growth performance will be significantly restricted.

Second, the Southeast has two separate and distinct labor markets. In the southern portion of the South Atlantic states, participation rates have approached national norms, occupational distributions are even more centered in white-collar activities than in the nation, and employment in the trade and service sectors is slightly above national concentration rates. In the East South Central, however, all the above factors are significantly lower than nationwide. Moreover, the industrial base of this region appears to be eroding very rapidly. Thus, the Southeast may be slowly dividing into a rapid-growth and a slow-growth sector.

Third, new manufacturing industries that are expected to expand rapidly in the 1980s are not becoming more important in the South than in the nation. Unless this trend is altered, the growth of basic industry in this region must slow.

Fourth, the importance of government purchases to the Southeast region have been overstated. Indeed, total per capita expenditures by the federal government fall short of national norms. While military personnel residing in the continental United States are 30 percent more heavily concentrated in the Southeast than in the nation, they are concentrated in military bases that are designed to train new personnel. Thus, many of the military are not the recipients of high wages. Although military procurement is expected to aid expansion in central Florida, the Atlanta suburbs, and northern Alabama, the region as a whole is not expected to receive the same amount of per capita procurement dollars as the nation.

Fifth, the occupational distribution by race differs dramatically in the Southeast. White-collar workers are white, while blue-collar workers are black. Although black unemployment rates in the region remain below those nationwide, this mismatch of occupational characteristics by race suggests that the unemployment differential between races may widen as blue-collar jobs become relatively scarce.

This chapter will attempt to address these problems and others associated with differential participation rates and educational skills and will attempt to devise projections of employment conditions in 1990. While the conclusions will remain relatively sketchy, this attempt to project developments forward is expected to uncover areas of unemployment stress that may be useful for planners concerned about the region during the remainder of this decade.

Employment Growth Aided by Natural Convergence

Theoretically, regional imbalances are expected to gradually disappear as changing factor incomes and changing migration eliminate economic differentials. For example, the low wages that prevail in the Southeast should encourage expansion of productive resources. This industrial expansion, in turn, should lead to increased employment and a gradual reduction in wage discrepancies. Normally, the low-wage region exhibits significant underemployment of labor resources, reflected in low participation rates and high unemployment rates while this process is developing. At the same time, labor is expected to migrate from the low-earning areas. In fact, unemployment rates in the Southeast have normally remained well below those in the nation. Also, population movements have been favorable to the Southeast. The attractiveness of retirement in Florida clearly has been a factor in this migration pattern, but employment growth also has been significant in the Carolinas, Georgia, and even in the Gulf Coast counties of Alabama and Mississippi. Although high wages have influenced migration patterns to the Gulf Coast, wages appear not to have been influential in slowing population movements.

Apparently, labor markets in the Southeast are much more stratified than migration theory would suggest. As manufacturing began to lose world markets and became exposed to imported materials, jobs began to disappear in textiles and apparel, chemicals and rubber, and the metals and shipbuilding industries in Alabama and Mississippi. Except in the latter instances, the jobs that were lost were low-wage occupations. In the meantime, the return to the South of the lumber industry, the increase in durable manufacturing related to electronics, and the greater need for distribution to provide for the growing population in Florida prevented the Southeast markets from eroding relative to the nation. As a result, the fast-foods, shopping malls, and other infrastructure that were widely accepted nationwide came to the South.

Much of the more rapid employment growth in the Southeast was contributed by trade, transportation, and financial activity. While the finance group and services remain less concentrated in the Southeast than nationwide, all the service sectors have grown nearly 30 percent more rapidly than in the nation during the last decade. To the extent that these growth rates were created by convergence of activity to conform to homogeneous tastes among the regions, this rapid employment growth will not persist in the future.

Of course, some of the expansion in services and trade reflects increased wholesaling and convention-related lodging that can be more appropriately classified as basic activity than as infrastructure. To a large extent, however, more rapid expansion in transportation services, finance, and private services in the Southeast reflects a one-time adjustment to a pattern of services that has become standard throughout all the regions of the nation.

If much of the more rapid growth in employment in the Southeast during the 1970s represented this one-time convergence toward a homogeneous set of service activities, then growth rates should be expected to slow in the absence of improved comparative advantage for basic industries in this region. In fact, changes in construction employment suggest just that possibility. While construction employment expanded more rapidly in the South than nationwide (3.0 percent versus 2.6 percent during the decade), construction has actually declined slightly relative to the nation in the last five years. These declines have been especially abrupt in Florida, Georgia, and North Carolina—three states that have been experiencing rapid but slowly declining rates of expansion. According to a regional formula that was estimated several years ago, construction only needs to utilize about 2.5 percent of the work force in order to maintain a constant level of roads and facilities (assuming that the relationship between those facilities and the employment base remains constant). Every single percentage point gain in employment requires slightly more than a percentage point gain in construction activity and, therefore, in construction employment. If that formulation is generally valid, construction employment over time becomes a barometer of anticipated employment growth. While that barometer is not yet saying that growth in the Southeast will fall below projected growth rates for the nation, it definitely is indicating that growth in the Southeast during the next ten years will be decidedly slower, possibly as much as a full percentage point per year slower than in the past decade. If so, employment in the Southeast may expand only at an annual rate of 2.5 percent for the remainder of the decade, as compared to the 3.7 percent annual growth rate in the previous decade. In general, the growth rates appear to be slowing more in the previously fast-growing states throughout the entire region. This is expected to continue.

No Convergence Apparent in East South Central Region

Although the previous discussion treats conditions for the region as a whole, available data clearly show that the East South Central states of Alabama, Mississippi, Tennessee, and Kentucky are considerably different from their East Coast neighbors. These states have a heavier concentration of high-wage manufacturing and mining than do the other parts of the Southeast. While textiles and apparel are diminishing along the Atlantic, mining and metal fabrication and production are slumping in the South Central region. The loss of high-wage jobs apparently has not been able to preserve the purchasing power of that part of the Southeast. Therefore, infrastructure expansion has not taken place. The location quotients for transportation services, finance, and private services are the lowest concentrations of those activities in all the census regions of the nation.

Population growth rates remain mixed in that region as Tennessee continues to attract people, while most areas of Mississippi and Alabama lose them either to their own Gulf Coast counties or to Tennessee and surrounding states.

Participation rates are notoriously low throughout those four states, with female participation rates remaining the lowest of all census regions. Moreover, there has been no evidence of convergence, primarily because the sluggish growth of service activity has not opened up opportunities for females. In addition, the characteristics of the higher wage durable manufacturing industries has not attracted secondary workers into the labor market. Finally, the very high unemployment rates in that region, among the highest in the nation, also have influenced the current low participation rates.

No region has a smaller concentration of white-collar workers and a higher concentration of blue-collar workers than the East South Central region. While 53 percent of all jobs in the United States are white collar, only 45 percent of jobs in this region are white collar. White collar jobs are more scarce not only in the managerial and sales areas but also for clerical workers. Indeed, even women in that region have a smaller concentration in the clerical areas than in any other region in the country. The highest concentration of blue-collar workers was in nondurable operative jobs. As many of those jobs have been rapidly vanishing because of the current recession, unemployment has risen sharply. Unlike the Midwest, where many workers appear to have priced themselves out of their jobs, employment problems in the East South Central region appear to be related to a mismatch of low-quality job skills.

For the purposes of this discussion, the interesting question is why convergence is not developing in the East South Central region. Part of the explanation may be that the heavy concentration of blue-collar skills diminishes the desires of the population to attain the same level of trade and private services that prevail in all parts of the country. Of course, the recent loss of these manufacturing jobs can only reduce the market pressures to develop the trade and private service infrastructure. In the absence of new basic industries developing in this region, an actual decline in employment is possible.

More likely, the East South Central region will experience below-average employment growth, ultimately leading to below-average population growth. The stagnant performance of the 1950s and 1960s may replace the spurt of the 1970s. Of course, such an employment performance in a region that already had relatively low participation rates certainly will lead to prolonged periods of unusually high unemployment rates. As the Southeast region as a whole is not expected to deviate significantly from the nation, the South Atlantic states will need to perform well above average to offset this area of weak development. However, higher unemployment in states contiguous to states that are generating increasing jobs almost certainly will generate some migration of unemployed families. Of course, the jobs being created in the South Atlantic will continue to be concentrated in the service industries and white-collar occupations. Thus, the ability to employ the blue-collar nondurable operatives who have been laid off because of mill closings will be significantly reduced. Nevertheless, the readily available influx of experienced, if not appropriately skilled, workers from areas of geographical proximity assures that wages will not accelerate unduly and that unemployment will not fall dramatically below national averages in the South Atlantic states.

Growth for Basic Industries

If the Southeast region remains as effective in attracting basic industries in the next decade as it did in the previous decade, the occupational imbalances in the East South Central region and the convergence of employment concentrations suggest that employment opportunities in the Southeast must grow more slowly. However, slow growth is not inevitable. Changing competitive positions in the region could attract new industries, leading to much more rapid expansion than appears likely.

As the Southeast began to grow in population and increase its per capita incomes, regional markets became large enough to support the production of goods that previously were demanded in the region but supplied elsewhere. This import substitution accounts for much of the growth in manufacturing (other than the textile/apparel area) between 1960 and 1980. For example, food processing, printing, and metal fabrication all sharply improved their employment concentrations over that period of time.

At the present time, one major industry in the Southeast continues to recede—the textile industry. The number of employees working in broadcloth mills has decreased by more than 30,000 since the beginning of this decade. Most of this job decay is related to permanent replacement by foreign suppliers. On the other hand, the building materials industry has staged a remarkable comeback in the region. Between 1950 and 1970, employment in the lumber, furniture, and stone and related industries actually declined. Gains reappeared during the 1970s and are continuing today. Some of the new industries, such as communications, computer technology, and control systems, have developed concentrations in central Florida, Atlanta, and the research triangle in Huntsville, Alabama. Even as other durable manufacturing slumped into recession, employment in electrical machinery, which incorporates many of these industries, actually increased slightly in 1982. Employment also increased for other durables, including scientific instruments and ordnance. While the relatively rapid rate of growth of these industries is encouraging, their size in the region remains relatively small. In addition, questions remain about the ability of the regional educational systems to provide necessary skilled personnel to preserve reasonable employment growth in these industries without creating undue wage pressures.

Currently, employment trends in the Southeast do not indicate that this region will obtain its share of defense growth industries in the next decade. This would suggest that the growth of employment in basic industries will slow. Combined with the other observations on occupational distortions and convergence, this would certainly imply that no new areas of rapid growth exist in the region.

While such a conclusion may be justified, the definition of basic industries must first be expanded. Partially because Florida is an attraction for tourists, the restaurant, hostelry, and recreational services provided for visitors from other regions should be included in basic industries. (Note, it is the attainment of purchasing power from *outside* the region that determines a basic industry, not the mere fact that it provides services for tourists. Florida facilities that attract vacationing Alabamans are part of the Southeast region infrastructure rather than one of its basic industries.) Of course, such service-providing industries must be viewed in terms of their net effect on attracting external purchasing power. If more southerners seek vacations outside of this region, and spend more there than nonsouthern tourists spend on vacations in the Southeast, then tourism does not provide growth for the southern economy. The evidence that is available strongly suggests, however, that the balances are heavily in favor of the Southeast.

Purchasing power also aids southern growth when households move from other regions with their accumulated savings and spend from their wealth holdings after they come south. Florida unquestionably benefits greatly from this capital flow that migrates with retiring families. Coastal developments along the Atlantic and Gulf also benefit by such interregional flows in savings. No firm evidence exists to measure the net effect of these capital flows on the South. The result of one study that found capital flows to the South were surprisingly large (40 percent of all regional investment appears to be financed by nonregional funds) implies that this imported purchasing power remains a significant engine of southeastern growth. Governmental flows through Social Security and related programs also have aided development in parts of the South.

No clear estimates can be made about the potential for developing basic industries in the Southeast during the next ten years. Import substitution almost certainly is slowing in the manufacturing sector. While some other manufacturing activity is expanding rapidly, most of the projected gains in electrical machinery, other durables, and related industries will be offset by continuing decay in the textile industry. Growth of those basic industries in the service sectors, such as net gains from tourism, may continue at nearly the rate of expansion of the last ten years. Moreover, the interregional transfers of household capital, which appear to benefit developments in parts of the South, should continue to grow, although transfers through Social Security disbursements may not be increasing as favorably in the 1980s as in the 1970s because of Social Security reform. On balance, the regional engines of growth as measured by gains in basic industries should be no stronger in the next ten years than in the past ten years and may be modestly less robust. Combined with previous observations, this confirms that employment growth in the Southeast almost certainly will slow by a full percentage point by 1990.

Government Influence

Almost a decade ago the infamous economic war between the states was launched by an article in the *National Tax Journal* asserting that allocation formulas on government grants significantly favored the South. To be sure, some vestiges of southern economic development that were instituted during the administration of

Franklin Roosevelt remained. The most visible of these was the Appalachian Commission and the Tennessee Valley Authority. Because of previous efforts by powerful southern politicians, many military training bases were established in their districts, although the climate requirements of those bases probably would have led to significant placement in the South anyway. Approximately one-third of all resident military are assigned to the Southeast, a proportion that greatly exceeds its concentration of population and economic power.

Clearly the progressive tax system has been a factor in aiding the relative development of the South. Prices are lower in rural areas, and housing costs have traditionally been lower in the South. Geographic studies of relative prices show a ten percentage point differential between the Southeast and the national norm. Therefore, the marginal tax rate paid on a constant dollar of purchasing power is slightly less in the South than in other parts of the country.

Furthermore, the median tax in the Southeast is about four percentage points lower than nationwide, at least partially because earnings are lower even after adjustment for inflation. (Remember, the average wage in the South is 19 percent below the national norms while the inflation rate appears to be only 10 percent reduced.) Furthermore, a higher incidence of poverty exists in the Southeast than in the nation as a whole. Programs designed to aid those in poverty certainly would be more heavily disbursed in this region than in other parts of the country. To no one's surprise, Mississippi is a substantial net recipient of resources from the federal government. As the state having the highest incidence of poverty in the United States and the lowest per capita incomes, even after adjustment for inflation, should that fact be surprising?

What is surprising, however, is the fact that despite these transfers and tax considerations, most southern states receive less from the federal government than they pay into their coffers. States such as Tennessee, Georgia, and the Carolinas rank in the middle of all states receiving outlays per capita from federal resources. Indeed, a close examination of the claim that the South receives a dis-proportionate share of government money rests on the fact that the District of Columbia resides in the census region of the South and the military and social programs are disbursed in the District's suburbs in Virginia and Maryland. Most southern states contribute to the development of that administrative network along with other states in the country. If the District of Columbia and Maryland could be added to the Northeast region with which they have closer economic ties than with the South, then the discrepancies in allocations of government programs would be virtually eliminated.

Moreover, the actual concentration of transfer payments among regions and the actual differential in progressive tax payments does not indicate how those forces are changing. Some of the allocation formulas have altered to conform more closely with population concentrations than needs. As a result, relative flows of federal resources to the South have diminished. More substantially, nonretirement transfer programs and intergovernmental grants as a proportion of economic activity have recently been reduced. In addition, recent tax reductions have significantly reduced the tax payment differential between regions. Finally, inflation rates appear to have accelerated slightly in the South in comparison to other parts of the country. Housing costs, in particular, have become more closely related to national costs.

All of the changes just mentioned are leading to less relative support from government activities than previously had been available. There are two offsets to this trend. First, transfer payments to retirees have increased relative to economic activity, and represent a higher-than-national concentration along the southeastern coasts and in Florida. Second, the volunteer Army in the latter 1970s led to a significant gain in purchasing power for the military personnel residing in this region. That gain has diminished in recent years. It should be noted that a heavy concentration of military personnel does not mean a heavy concentration of the increased military purchases that currently are developing. Except for Huntsville (Alabama), Pascagoula (Mississippi), Marietta (Georgia), and subcontractors in central Florida, the military buildup is bypassing the South. Indeed, the region may be a net contributor rather than a net recipient of the defense buildup. This is especially true if the buildup of materials continues to be partially financed by a restraint on the salaries received by military personnel.

The previous observations strongly suggest that the federal

government is a diminishing force in the economic development of the Southeast. Indeed, it is not unusual to observe a decline in the concentration of federal employees in many of the smaller metropolitan areas in this region that are contiguous to military bases. The good news is that private activity has been generated to offset the diminishing influence of federal activity. The bad news is that the relative importance of federal activity in those metropolitan areas may continue to diminish. Once again the federal presence in the South is not an engine of growth but rather an engine of restraint on southern development, with several notable exceptions.

The Cyclical Responsiveness of Wages

In a paper written several years ago, Robert Hall claimed that the noncyclical wage payments of the federal government had a significant stabilizing impact on wages in the private sector in those communities where government payrolls were heavily concentrated. Certainly, wages paid in the shipyards on the Gulf Coast appear to have distorted surrounding wage contracts. However, a test of the Hall hypothesis on the mill towns has not been conducted.

If his hypothesis is confirmed, the degree of wage stickiness that such conditions would generate could increase the cyclicality of employment in those towns. A study by the Department of Commerce definitely indicates that cyclicality has increased in the Southeast, although a part of that fluctuation may have been created by heavier relative concentrations in durable manufacturing than in the past. Not enough information is currently available to determine whether the cyclical responsiveness of wages is lower in the South than nationwide.

However, the minimum wage increases in the late 1970s appear to have had a slightly adverse effect on the market responsiveness of southern wages. Now that further additions to minimum wage legislation have been delayed, southern wages may become more responsive to changing economic conditions. As a result, employment in the South may become slightly less responsive to cyclicality, while the relative competitiveness of southern industry may improve. All of these assertions are speculative, but some fleeting evidence suggests that they are appropriate.

More on Occupational Distributions

The significant difference in the distribution of employment among occupations between the East South Central region and the remainder of the South has already been discussed. As mentioned earlier, the East South Central region has the greatest dispersion from national norms in its occupational profile. In general, the South Atlantic states have comparable occupational profiles to those available nationwide. To that extent, structural unemployment should be less intense in the South Atlantic states than in the East South Central states.

However, the occupational profile shows dramatic differences between blacks and whites in the South Atlantic. Because the white population has the same blue-collar concentration as blacks in the East South Central region, the dispersion between the two races is not very great. In the South Atlantic region, by way of contrast, whites have a high concentration of sales and managerial positions, while blacks have the second lowest concentration relative to other regions in the country. As a result, the differential between white and black occupation profiles is the largest in the South Atlantic of all regions in the country. Migration patterns may explain the reasons for this significant differential. The largest concentration of blacks in the United States remains in the Southeast and especially in the East South Central region. As jobs have vanished in the East South Central region, blacks have migrated to the South Atlantic region. Unfortunately, they have arrived with the same skills that proved to be unemployable in their old region. Therefore, they have not been easily integrated into the available employment opportunities of the South Atlantic area.

At the same time, employment opportunities in sales and managerial positions have encouraged migration from outside the region into the South Atlantic. Although these jobs are not as high paying in the Southeast as in the nation, they are positions that normally profit from growing market conditions. Therefore, the potential opportunity exists to provide compensation that may not be available elsewhere. Thus, the Southeast is creating jobs for people trained in the Midwest and Northeast, while continuing to disemploy the high concentration of blue-collar workers indigenous to the Southeast. By 1990 the United States should provide white-collar jobs for more than 55 percent of its workers. The South Atlantic will have converged on that average by then. Professional and technical job concentrations probably will be approaching 17 percent, even though teaching positions will slightly decline. Most of this growth will be at the expense of blue-collar operatives (e.g., assemblers and machine operators), especially in nondurable goods manufacturing. As a result of these changes, there are not expected to be any more absolute blue-collar jobs by the end of this decade than currently exist. Unless the black population changes its occupational skills, the gap between white and black unemployment, which has been narrower in this region than in the nation as a whole, will widen to and above national norms. In short, the ability to attract jobs commensurate with the skill levels of the southeastern population are extremely limited. The challenge will be to create the job skills in the current work force that meet the developing needs of business firms.

Although any analysis of teenage employment by occupation must be extremely suspect, the current occupational distribution suggests that such redirection of skills (to white-collar jobs) is not currently developing. Indeed, a larger proportion of teenage jobs is in blue-collar work in this region than in any other region and has been increasing its relative share. Of course, teenagers will go where jobs are available and the heavy concentration of blue-collar jobs in this region suggests that they can be employed in those areas. However, the occupation profile shows that the experience being gained by teenagers is not in the industries that will be growing most rapidly in the latter part of this decade.

Surprisingly, the situation is not as bleak for women in terms of their occupational skills as for black males. At least in the South Atlantic, the concentration of female white-collar workers approaches national norms. More surprisingly, the proportion of females with jobs as administrators and managers is higher than the national average, although it lags considerably behind similar concentrations in the West. Of course, the faster population growth rates in the South result in a population that is younger and has a heavier concentration of teenagers than do other parts of the country. This means that teachers comprise a heavier concentration of the southern work force than in other parts of the nation. (Of course, it also means that government is growing more rapidly in the South to meet its educational commitments than in the nation as a whole.) Female employment in the South also is heavily concentrated in nondurable operative positions. Female work has been heavily concentrated in the textile and apparel industries and the participation rates of females are high in those states. Apparently, as jobs erode in those industries, females move to alternative occupations rather than withdraw from the work force.

Although the conventional wisdom is that female employment remains largely in textiles or in homemaking, the occupational profiles dramatically demonstrate that management-type occupations are the fastest-growing source of jobs available to women in the South. Indeed, the rate of change of such occupations for women is greater in this region than in other parts of the country and the level of concentration now is only exceeded by the West Coast. If these trends continue, and they certainly are expected to do so, the significance of women in the southeastern work force will be altered dramatically and women's rights will be much more strongly championed in the region than they now are.

Conclusion

Probably the primary conclusion of this discussion is that employment opportunities in the Southeast will grow much more slowly in the next decade than they did in the 1970s. Indeed, employment probably will slow from a 3.7 percent growth path to only a 2.5 percent growth path. Given the low participation rates that currently exist for women, a larger proportion of this employment slowing will be reflected in less population movement than normally would be expected. Of course, participation rates actually grew more slowly in the South than nationwide in the last decade as job opportunities for women in nondurable operative occupations began to dwindle.

The second conclusion of this paper is that most of this slowing in population movement and in employment opportunities will be concentrated in the East South Central region of the South. This particular region is experiencing a significant erosion in employment opportunities in its heavily concentrated blue-collar occupations. Indeed, the East South Central region has the greatest dispersion in occupations from national norms. As convergence of activities continues in other parts of the country, these occupational skills will become increasingly unattractive. Except for the Gulf Coast, where energy development, tourism, and retiree communities are altering the development patterns, the East South Central region may experience an extended period of stagnation until the occupational distribution is improved either by education or by migration patterns. To the extent that blue-collar workers will migrate out of that region into the South Atlantic, the effect will be to generate higher unemployment rates in the latter region and lower wage pressures in low-skilled occupations than otherwise would occur. As a result, the 18 percent discrepancy between the hourly wage earned by factory workers in the South and the wage earned nationwide may persist through the next decade.

At the present time, the gap between unemployment rates for whites and blacks is narrower in this region than in other parts of the country. Part of this is based on similar occupational distributions between whites and blacks in the East South Central region. In the South Atlantic region, the relative distributions of occupations between whites and blacks are larger than in any other region in the country. Moreover, blacks may migrate from the East South Central region if a period of relative stagnation indeed develops. Thus, the third conclusion is that disparities between the black and white communities in the South Atlantic states may widen in this decade.

Of course, such conclusions are based on prevailing occupational skills. An examination of teenage occupational performance suggests that skills are not currently being developed. Apparently, teenagers migrate to jobs which are most heavily concentrated, even if those jobs are dwindling in importance. Thus, the teenagers in this region are receiving experience from jobs that will not be in the growth industries of the late 1980s. Obviously, educational programs can be designed to partially redress this problem of gaining work experience.

A surprising conclusion is that even as females have left

nondurable operative positions they appear to have sharply increased their concentration in managerial and administrative positions. Currently, southern females have the second highest concentration in that skill level of females throughout the nation. Only the West Coast shows higher managerial concentrations for females. Moreover, the distribution in this category has grown much more rapidly in the South than in the nation. If these trends continue, and they are expected to do so, the female labor force will become more professional and more influential in the South during this decade.

While unionization is not significant in any state of the South, the decline in union members as a percentage of the total employment picture has been slower in this region than in other parts of the nation. In Alabama, union members continue to constitute 19 percent of the work force, a concentration that was attained twenty years ago. Unfortunately, work stoppages are more heavily concentrated in those states which are most heavily unionized. This apparent militancy not only hardens the aim of managements to withstand unionization, but it also reduces the relative competitiveness of those industries. With unionization much heavier in the East South Central region and much lighter in the South Atlantic region, the labor movement should face considerable difficulty in gaining new members if stagnation is created in East South Central areas.

In general, unemployment rates are expected to be higher in the Southeast during the 1980s than in the 1970s. Population movements are expected to slow from an annual rate of 1.6 percent to an annual rate of about 1.3 percent. As mentioned earlier, employment growth also is expected to slow, although the burden of that slowing will be felt only in a subsector of the region. Regional disparities may widen rather than narrow, even as the South Atlantic converges on national norms.

In short, employment conditions in this region will generate many more challenges in the 1980s than existed during the booming periods of the late 1960s and the decade of the 1970s. Those challenges easily could be overcome, and the ability to attract new basic industries may increase. The Southeast, especially the South Atlantic states, have achieved significant gains in electrical machinery and scientific industries. However, the trends in government procurement, tax changes, and changes in transfer payments are not conducive to economic development in this region.

CHAPTER THREE

Prospects for Southeastern Employment Growth in the 1980s

RONALD ROBINSON

Vice President, Trust Company Bank,
Atlanta, Georgia

Introduction

Fundamental to the economic vitality of any region is the creation of adequate employment opportunities. The Southeast during the decade of the 1970s experienced rapid growth in both population and manufacturing jobs. An agrarian economy, which lasted until after World War II, has been replaced by manufacturing. The industrialization of the region has stemmed past problems of out-migration and lack of job opportunities.

Today, the Southeast is well into the eighties. Will this decade see a continuation of the employment gains made in recent years? This discussion will address some of the issues affecting the region's industrial development and employment growth. It will examine the economic history and the factors involved in the manufacturing growth of the Southeast. An attempt will also be made to predict future employment trends and challenges that must be faced if the region is to realize fully the value of its own "industrial revolution."

Economic Heritage of the Southeast

For the purpose of this study, the Southeast is defined as the states of North Carolina, South Carolina, Florida, Alabama, Mississippi, Tennessee, and Georgia. This collection of states possesses a unique economic heritage. As part of the Sunbelt, these states have exhibited strong economic growth, in contrast to those in the frost belt, which have experienced a relative decline, such as New York and many of the other traditional northeastern and midwestern industrial areas. This has initiated references to "The Second War Between the States," to be fought not by soldiers, but by economic developers. The spoils of this war are the expanding and relocating industrial facilities of this nation.

This point is of interest in its historical perspective. Who would have been farsighted enough in the pre-World War II South to have predicted that this region would, in only thirty years, pull itself from the depths of an economic disaster and be considered by the Midwest and Northeast as a threat to their economic well-being?

The War Between the States was a turning point for the agrarian South. The states forming the Confederacy suddenly found their wealth destroyed and much of their commerce in the hands of northern interests. In 1868, more than 95 percent of all southern railroads were owned by northern investors. With no previous industrial base to grow from and with impediments established to assure that a new base would not be established, the South existed in an economic environment of small-farm agriculture until after World War II. In 1888, The Interstate Commerce Commission established the differential freight rate system for railroads, which discriminated against the South and—for all practical purposes— guaranteed that the South would remain a supplier of agricultural raw materials for the use of northern industry.[1]

Cotton was "king," but this one-crop economy was a fragile one that kept the South in a small-farm economy and near the bottom of all economic measures. So desperate were the economic conditions in the South that the Great Depression was viewed by some as "only ten more years for the same thing we had known before."[2] In 1929, per capita income in Georgia was $349, which represented only 49.5 percent of the United States average. This was a decline from the 1919 levels that typified the boom years of cotton, when per capita income was $417, or 64 percent of the United States average.[3] This decline of an already depressed economy continued until after World War II. Then, in 1953, by order of the United States Supreme Court, the differential freight rate was eliminated. Most economic developers point to this major development as the catalyst for the period of growth in the South that has continued at an ever-increasing pace for the last thirty years.

All was not bleak for the economy of the Southeast during the period between Reconstruction and World War II, for foundations were being built for the postwar industrial boom. Railroads had expanded and connected the Southeast to other areas of the country. Even by the late 1800s the textile industry was reestablished in the region, as well as the iron and steel industries, principally in Alabama. The food processing and forest products industries were also adding to a small but growing manufacturing base.[4] The New England textile industry, encountering competitive difficulties, moved to the Southeast in the early part of this century, seeking people and waterpower. It found both of these ingredients in the Piedmont Crescent of North Carolina, South Carolina, and Georgia. World War II brought about increased demands for military equipment and supplies. This war-time economy accelerated both the rate of growth and diversification of the Southeast's industry.

Post-World War II Trends

Since World War II, the Southeast has undergone a dramatic change in its economic makeup. Even as late as 1940, agriculture remained the Southeast's principal industry. However, a continued erosion in the competitiveness of the region's agricultural base has led to the advent of a manufacturing economy.

Per Capita Income

From 1950 to 1970, per capita income in Georgia increased from $1,034 to $3,354 and, expressed as a percentage of United States per capita income, rose from 70.6 percent to 85.2 percent. By 1979, it had risen to 87 percent. This increase closely parallels that of the Southeast per capita income, which in 1979 was 86 percent of the United States average. These impressive per capita income growth figures reflect the changes occurring in the areas of population, total personal income, and employment.

Population Changes

One of the notable characteristics of the 1980 census figures in Exhibit 1 is that the South is the largest of the four regional divisions of the United States with some 75 million people. The Southeast, which includes states represented in both the South Central and South Atlantic census regions, is the fourth most populous of the eight census subdivisions. It is significant that not only is the Southeast one of the larger populated regions in this country, but as Exhibit 2 indicates, it also ranked number one in population growth in the ten years from 1970 to 1980. The rapid population expansion during this decade equates to a fast-growing and maturing market that is successfully competing with traditional industrial centers of the Northeast and Midwest.

This growth is phenomenal in light of the fact that the region had consistently lost population through internal migration during all of this century. Only beginning in the 1960s did out-migration begin to reverse itself.[5] While an exodus from agriculture was the primary reason for the extensive out-migration pattern of the 1950s, the result was the birth of active industrial development efforts at the state level, such as Mississippi's "Balance Agriculture with Industry" program. These state programs aimed to slow out-migration by replacing lost agricultural employment with manufacturing job opportunities. Combined with the aforementioned

Exhibit 1: **U.S. Population by Region and Division, 1980**

Region	Population
Northeast	
New England	12,300,000
Middle Atlantic	36,800,000
Total	49,100,000
North Central	
East North Central	41,700,000
West North Central	17,200,000
Total	58,900,000
South	
Southeast	35,200,000
Other South	40,100,000
Total	75,300,000
West	
Mountain	11,400,000
Pacific	31,800,000
Total	43,200,000

Source: *1980 Census of Population and Housing*, U.S. Department of Commerce, Bureau of the Census (Washington, D.C.: Government Printing Office).

elimination of the railroads' differential freight rate, these industrial development programs created an impetus through the 1960s and 1970s that has dramatically changed the economic and employment picture in this region.

Manufacturing Economy

In a relatively short period of time, the Southeast has evolved from an agrarian economy to a manufacturing-based economy. In 1940, employment in agriculture in the South was 73 percent above the national average, while in manufacturing, employment was approximately 33 percent below the national average.[6] By 1975, southern manufacturing employment lagged by only 10 percent, while the agricultural employment percentage equaled the national

Exhibit 2: **Regional Population Growth, 1970–1980**

Region	Change in numbers	Rank	Percentage change	Rank
Southeast	+6,557,505	1	+22.9%	2
Pacific	+5,244,527	2	+19.8	4
West South Central	+4,417,057	3	+22.9	3
Mountain	+3,078,429	4	+37.1	1
Other South	+1,561,613	5	+10.5	5
East North Central	+1,407,018	6	+ 3.5	8
West North Central	+ 760,519	7	+ 4.6	6
New England	+ 501,248	8	+ 4.2	7
Middle Atlantic	− 425,095	9	− 1.1	9

Source: Bethel W. Minter, "The Growth and Structure of the Economy of the Southeastern U.S." (Presentation to the first Armand G. Erpf Invitational Symposium on American Enterprise, Berry College, Mt. Berry, Georgia, 4 May 1981.)

average. In 1980, the percentage of manufacturing employment in the southeastern states actually exceeded the national average by 2.3 percent.

Between 1970 and 1980, manufacturing employment in the Southeast grew at more than three times the rate of the United States as a whole (Exhibit 3). Durable goods manufacturing continues to lag national averages, but changes are occurring. Evidence of this is the much stronger durable goods growth of 29.2 percent, compared to a national rate of only 9 percent. While traditional nondurable goods employment continued to show positive growth in the Southeast during the decade of the 1970s, durable goods employment growth outstripped it by more than three times.

The industry mix of the region (Exhibit 4) again reveals a heavy concentration in nondurable goods manufacturing such as textiles, apparel, and food. These industries have historically been more labor-intensive than durable goods production, which has a tendency to be more capital-intensive. Of the 3 million people in the Southeast's total manufacturing work force, almost 2 million

Exhibit 3: Civilian Nonfarm Employment

Employer	Percentage of total in 1980		Percentage change 1970-80	
	South-east	United States	South-east	United States
Manufacturing	24.8%	22.5%	16.3%	5.1%
Durable goods	10.5	13.5	29.2	9.0
Nondurable goods	14.3	9.0	8.3	- 0.1
Mining	0.5	1.1	43.1	64.5
Contract construction	5.7	4.9	38.4	24.6
Transportation, communications, utilities	5.5	5.7	33.8	14.2
Trade	22.2	22.7	53.0	36.8
Retail	16.5	16.9	53.0	38.4
Wholesale	5.7	5.8	53.1	32.3
Finance, insurance, real estate	5.1	5.7	57.8	41.6
Services	17.2	19.6	78.3	53.6
Government	19.0	17.8	49.4	28.8
Federal	3.3	3.2	19.2	4.9
State and local	15.7	14.7	57.9	35.4
Total	100.0%	100.0%	42.8%	27.9%

Source: Bethel W. Minter, "The Growth and Structure of the Economy of the Southeastern U.S." (Presentation to the first Armand G. Erpf Invitational Symposium on American Enterprise, Berry College, Mt. Berry, Georgia, 4 May 1981.)

are involved in the manufacture of nondurables, while more than 1.2 million are employed in the production of durable goods.

In 1980, the Southeast had 67.4 percent of the United States' manufacturing employment in textiles, 31.2 percent in apparel, 31.1 percent in furniture, and 25.1 percent in lumber (Exhibit 5). These industries may be defined as above-average in employment concentration. They all possess a percentage of employment greater than 16.1 percent, which is the percentage of total

Exhibit 4: **Southeastern Manufacturing Employment, January 1982**

SIC/Industry	Employment in Southeast (in thousands)
22 Textiles	540.7
23 Apparel	394.3
20 Food	256.1
36 Electric machinery	235.6
35 Nonelectric machinery	201.9
28 Chemicals	190.1
37 Transportation equipment	175.3
24 Lumber	157.3
34 Fabricated metals	156.0
25 Furniture	146.1
27 Printing	144.9
26 Paper	125.0
30 Rubber/plastics	102.8
33 Primary metals	101.6
39 Miscellaneous manufacturing	92.8
32 Stone/clay/glass	89.9
38 Instruments	29.0
31 Leather	27.4
29 Petroleum	4.0
21 Tobacco	3.8
Total manufacturing	3,174.6
Durable goods	1,292.7
Nondurable goods	1,881.9

Source: Atlanta Office, Bureau of Labor Statistics, U.S. Department of Labor and various published totals from the *Labor Market Trends* of the Southeast states.

manufacturing employment in the Southeast compared to the United States. All of these industries with above-average employment concentration, except textiles, experienced higher growth rates in the Southeast than they did nationwide from 1970 to 1980.

Exhibit 5: Industries of Above-average Concentration in Southeast

Industry	Southeast as percentage of United States, 1980	Change: 1970–80 United States	Southeast
Textiles	67.4%	–11.4%	– 7.9%
Apparel	31.2	– 4.8	11.5
Furniture	31.1	6.3	15.6
Lumber	25.1	7.7	15.8
Paper	17.9	– 1.7	10.2
Chemicals	17.7	6.1	18.8
Food and tobacco	16.3	– 6.0	5.8
Above-average group	27.8	– 2.3	5.1
Total manufacturing	16.1	5.1	16.3

Source: Bethel W. Minter, "The Growth and Structure of the Economy of the Southeastern U.S." (Presentation to the first Armand G. Erpf Invitational Symposium on American Enterprise, Berry College, Mt. Berry, Georgia, 4 May 1981.)

Even in textiles, where there was a decline of 11.4 percent nationally, the regional decline was only 7.9 percent. Apparel had a national decline of 4.8 percent but a regional growth of 11.5 percent. Overall, the above-average group exhibited a ten-year growth rate of 5.1 percent, while this same group declined in employment nationally by 2.3 percent.

The industries of below-average employment concentration in the Southeast (Exhibit 6), or those with less than 16.1 percent, showed a ten-year growth rate of 36.6 percent. Machinery, for instance, grew by 65 percent. The growth of the below-average group is more than seven times that of the above-average industries. These figures define a shift that is taking place in southeastern manufacturing employment away from a heavy dependence on consumer goods, such as textiles and apparel, to a more diversified manufacturing mix. It is also significant that in all fourteen industry sectors the Southeast outperformed the United States as a whole.

Exhibit 6: **Industries of Below-average Concentration in Southeast**

Industry	Southeast as percentage of United States, 1980	Change: 1970-80	
		United States	Southeast
Total manufacturing	16.1%	5.1%	16.3%
Stone/clay/glass	14.9	3.7	17.9
Unclassified nondurables	14.0	5.3	47.3
Printing and publishing	10.6	15.2	46.7
Machinery	9.6	19.7	65.0
Metals	9.3	- 2.1	23.2
Unclassified durables	9.3	17.7	27.5
Transportation equipment	8.8	2.0	14.4
Below-average group	10.1	9.4	36.6

Source: Bethel W. Minter, "The Growth and Structure of the Economy of the Southeastern U.S." (Presentation to the first Armand G. Erpf Invitational Symposium on American Enterprise, Berry College, Mt. Berry, Georgia, 4 May 1981.)

Factors in Manufacturing Growth of the Region

It is obvious from the data presented thus far that the southeastern region is going through a remarkable industrialization process that will never be witnessed again in this country. The Southeast can probably be accurately characterized as the last frontier of industrial development in the United States.

To recognize this phenomenon is relatively easy, but to analyze the factors that are fueling the industrialization process is more complicated. The complication arises because these factors not only vary throughout the evolutionary industrial development process but also vary in significance from industry to industry.

In a recent study by the Federal Reserve Bank of Atlanta, industries that had located a new plant or expanded an existing facility in Virginia, North Carolina, or South Carolina were asked to rank their business location decision factors. The top five factors listed were (1) state/local industrial climate, (2) labor productivity, (3) transportation, (4) land availability and room for expansion, and (5) cost of land and construction. The study cites a similar national poll by *Fortune* magazine in 1977 listing the top five plant location factors as transportation, proximity to customers, unskilled labor, energy supply, and productivity. The Federal Reserve Bank study generalizes the comparison of the two studies by saying that "firms come to this region for its lower overall production cost—from labor productivity, land and construction—and for its business climate. Nationally, on the other hand, most firms are more market-oriented, seeking good transportation and proximity to markets."[7]

In both studies, state financial inducements ranked relatively low. Long-term economic factors affecting the cost of doing business seem to be much more important in the facility location decision process. While proximity to markets was ranked only eleventh by the managers polled in the bank study, the population and industrial growth that has occurred in the Southeast over the last twenty years has, nevertheless, created a very vibrant market for all manner of consumer and industrial goods. This factor will be, therefore, increasingly important in future plant locations. Proximity to markets is particularly critical in the location of manufacturing support industries, such as heat treating, tool and die, and precision injection molding, which tend to lag the development of a primary industrial base.

Labor productivity (2) was ranked significantly ahead of wage rates (6) as a plant location factor. While cheap labor has been touted as a major reason for the industrial development of the Southeast, a more accurate analysis may well reveal that lower per-unit cost is a stronger attraction for this region.

It is a surprise to no one that state and local industrial climate is ranked as the number one location factor by the plant locators. To quote Maurice Fulton, former chairman of the Fantus Company: "The importance of business climate continues, [and] will continue, to be a major facility location factor. At the lowest common denominator, a favorable business climate is often a state of mind of a particular client toward a specific situation at a precise moment. Individual perceptions can be a dominant factor in excluding a candidate community or state from a facility location decision."[8] For the most part, the southern industrial developers have tried to project to the corporate community an environment of pro-business state and local governments, stable and equitable tax structures, and favorable labor/management relations. In short, industrial developers have presented the South as having an environment of cooperation, not confrontation. This has been borne out by manufacturing experience and continues to be a major reason for the region's economic growth.

Transportation is also a key to the continued success of the Southeast in its competition for job opportunities. The Southeast is blessed with an excellent multimodal transportation system. Deep water ports on both the Atlantic and Gulf coasts, newly completed interstate highways, profitable rail systems, and excellent air service, exemplified by Atlanta's Hartsfield International Airport, add up to an efficient, cost-effective transportation network.

The ease and cost of moving personnel, raw materials, and finished products was listed in the top five location criteria in both studies cited previously. Another study found that when a company is searching for a new manufacturing site three of the major criteria are transportation-related—proximity to markets, proximity to supplies or resources, and proximity to other company facilities.[9]

Future Trends

A discussion of the economic growth that has occurred in the southeastern United States raises the question of where the economy is going to be in the late 1980s. Can this growth be sustained? What direction will it take relative to manufacturing versus service sectors? Can the region compete for the emerging technology jobs? What are the impediments, and are there solutions? Many of these answers can be determined from the past makeup of the regional economy and its current status.

Today the Southeast is at an interesting plateau of development. It has come from an economy primarily based on agriculture to a secondary stage based on manufacturing. The regional manufacturing base is in transition from production of nondurable to durable goods, from labor-intensive to capital-intensive industries, and from dependence on basic consumer goods to a diversified industrial economy. Simultaneously, the region is progressing at a rapid pace toward a service-oriented economy.

Growth of Services

Services have lagged the manufacturing component, but there will be continued growth in this sector. In a speech given in October 1982 before the Southern Industrial Development Council, Governor Charles S. Robb of Virginia said, "There are basic changes at work within the structure of the American economy that promise to reshape our national work place."[10] One of the most interesting descriptions of these changes is offered by John Naisbit. In his recent book, *Megatrends,* Naisbit acknowledges that we're moving from an industrially oriented society to an information-based society, and he concludes that our future economic vigor will depend less on the goods we manufacture than on the information services we provide. As confirmation of that fact, in 1982 —for the first time in our history—a greater number of Americans found jobs in service industries than in manufacturing. I fully subscribe to the view that it is in the information and services industries that much of our future dynamic growth will occur, and it is on this sector of our economy that we are going to have to concentrate our development efforts.

Recent studies substantiate this trend of rapid growth in service industries. In 1979, service industries accounted for 19.4 percent of total national employment. By 1990, it is projected that this percentage will rise to 22 percent. Health care and related medical services will lead the way in this category.[11] Attending to the health care needs of a growing elderly population will create more job opportunities in hospitals and nursing homes. Other occupations, including food service and child care, should also exhibit rapid increases.

While Robb and many others feel that it is in the area of services that our future growth potential lies, it must be remembered that national trends may be diluted at the regional and community level. While the service industries demand attention from the industrial development community, this must be viewed within the context of an overall economic development program. As has already been pointed out, even traditional southern industries such as apparel are still growing in employment, and their impact cannot be ignored. There is a real danger in pursuing economic development myopically, for much of the growth in services is directly related to the increase in basic manufacturing employment. Only when wealth demands services does this sector flourish. The Southeast cannot afford to sacrifice the wealth-producing area of manufacturing that supports the growth of the service sector.

High Technology

The definition of high technology varies, depending on the person discussing the subject. Like "Sunbelt" it, too, has become a buzzword and is used very freely without a strict definition. Despite the lack of agreement on definition, most studies seem to point toward increased employment opportunities in the emerging technologies and competition for these jobs will be fierce as states and regions scramble to get their share.

As part of a series of papers focusing on the future of Georgia, Dr. Ross Hammond, then chief of the Industrial Development Division, Engineering Experiment Station, Georgia Institute of Technology, wrote: "The need for attracting high-technology industries has long been apparent. No less than three major reports of the Industrial Development Division of Georgia Tech have been devoted to pointing out the need for this effort.... All of these reports stress the type of industry which needs to be sought, such as electrical and nonelectrical machinery and primary and fabricated metals.... Chemicals and transportation equipment are two other industries which are also strong elements in many of the states which have higher per capita income."[12]

By Hammond's definition of high technology, the Southeast is already successful. Recalling the 65 percent growth rate in employment in machinery manufacture between 1970 and 1980, the region seems to be rapidly moving toward solving this need for high-technology jobs. However, many people today narrowly define high technology in terms of the electronics and biomedical industries and even suggest that perhaps emphasis should be placed solely on those industrial groups. At first glance, this may seem a highly desirable approach, particularly in light of the success of North Carolina's Research Triangle or the emerging electronics complex in central Florida. However, these opportunities should be pursued only within the context of an overall economic development effort that addresses a diversity of employment needs throughout the region.

The Southeast will see many new, more sophisticated, and highly technical industrial locations in the coming years. Competitive pressures will force further mechanization and automation in all industrial sectors. These changes will create a demand for a more highly trained labor force. This need for better educated and skilled employees may well be the single most important factor in determining the future of the southeastern economy.

Will the Southeast rise to this challenge facing our educational system? Can it? According to the Southern Growth Policies Board (1980 Commission on the Future of the South), "the need to improve the quality of education is recognized as being a prerequisite for attracting industry from which management and employees demand good schooling for their children. It is also necessary for training work forces to handle the increasingly sophisticated level of jobs that are opening up in services and manufacturing. Quality education is the only hope for the large adult population in the South, much of it in rural areas, who do not have the skills to earn a good living. Most importantly, it is the gift of the future for the southern children."[13]

The challenge is clear. A better educational system must be provided at all levels. There must be increased emphasis on fundamental skills (reading, writing, and computation in elementary schools), more emphasis on advanced mathematics and science in high schools, and a greater spirit of cooperation rather than competition among colleges and universities. Also, there is a need to reevaluate the technical and vocational systems that have served industrial development efforts so well in the past. Are they meeting today's needs? Are they teaching today's technology?

While the region can do little to actually influence the creation of products by high technology companies, it can continue to foster a business climate that is attractive and conducive to innovation. A major element in this environment is a labor force that has the advantages of advanced training and coordinated educational programs.

The immediate solution to these questions and challenges is to allocate more money, but money alone does not guarantee quality education. The technology of today applied to education may be the ultimate answer. Microcomputers and advanced communication systems provide the capability to spread educational resources statewide and even regionwide. By applying these technologies, opportunities for consistent, quality instruction can be made available to all citizens.

Existing Industry

Another opportunity for employment growth in the 1980s comes from the continued expansion of the region's existing manufacturing base. Each year a significant portion of new jobs comes from this source. In Georgia, during the five years from 1977 to 1981, 45.4 percent of the state's new manufacturing jobs came from the expansion of existing industries. The region's existing technology-oriented companies may also provide the solution for additional employment opportunities in high technology. By nurturing this existing technology base and promoting an environment conducive to growth, spin-offs from these existing facilities can develop a critical mass of advanced technology industry that will become self-sustaining.

The Southeast cannot afford to take its existing industry for granted. Competition for new jobs is increasing and other states are now coming to this region in attempts to lure away southern industry. More attention must be given to maintaining a climate for expansion and meeting the needs of existing employers. This effort should be complementary and not detrimental to the region's continuing programs to attract new industry.

Foreign Investment

Foreign investment is another factor within the changing economy of the Southeast that will have an increasing impact on employment opportunities in the 1980s. Within the last fifteen years, significant numbers of new international manufacturing facilities have opened in the United States. One major reason for this investment is the desire of foreign manufacturers to compete more effectively in the United States market. Second, trade barriers, either actual or threatened, have caused certain foreign industrial facilities to move to this country in order to protect historic market share. Third, the United States is generally viewed as the last bastion of the free enterprise system, and its economic and political stability make it attractive as a location for capital investments.

The Southeast continues to be a major benefactor in this movement of foreign capital and manufacturing jobs because the region remains the most attractive area for foreign investment in the United States.[14] One explanation for this attractiveness may be that the foreign investor is not tied either personally or professionally to any area of the country and, therefore, may make a more optimal location decision than a domestic investor. The major investing countries include the more developed and highly industrialized, with the United Kingdom ranked first in number of manufacturing facilities in this region (Exhibit 7). North Carolina and Georgia enjoy the largest number of facilities but all the region's states, except Mississippi, have significant investments.

Accompanying the manufacturing investment, particularly in and around Atlanta, is a major growth in international support services. Foreign consular corps offices, banking facilities, and chambers of commerce complement the direct air service from Atlanta to London, Frankfurt, Brussels, and Amsterdam that has been established only within the last six years. The impact of these foreign investments and services will certainly be a major factor to consider in the future employment growth of the Southeast.

Conclusion

The outlook for employment growth during the 1980s in the Southeast is bright. Growth rates in population and nonfarm employment are forecast to continue to outpace the United States as a whole. In the manufacturing sector, the fastest growing industries in the Southeast will not be those that have historically been the major employers. Machinery, both electrical and nonelectrical, is expected to show the largest increase in number of employees, followed by chemicals, rubber and plastics, and transportation equipment. Many sectors of these industries can certainly be categorized as high technology, particularly when compared to

Exhibit 7: **Location of Foreign-owned U.S. Manufacturers by Parent Countries, Selected States**

								States
Country	Ala.	Fla.	Ga.	Miss.	N.C.	S.C.	Tenn.	Total
United Kingdom	11	26	38	1	52	18	18	164
Federal Republic of Germany	6	20	12	3	47	31	14	133
Canada	8	15	18	5	22	8	9	85
France	5	8	17	–	4	10	1	45
Netherlands	1	8	5	–	18	6	7	45
Japan	2	5	15	–	7	6	3	38
Switzerland	3	1	1	–	6	11	6	28
Sweden	4	5	1	–	1	–	2	13
Belgium	–	1	5	–	2	2	3	13
South Africa	–	1	2	–	1	1	1	6
Austria	–	1	1	–	1	1	1	5
Denmark	–	1	1	–	1	–	–	3
Panama	–	2	–	–	–	–	1	3
Curacao	–	1	–	–	–	1	–	2
Finland	–	–	1	–	1	–	–	2
Italy	–	–	1	–	1	–	–	2
Saudi Arabia	1	–	–	–	–	–	–	1
Australia	–	1	–	–	–	–	–	1
Brazil	–	1	–	–	–	–	–	1
Norway	–	–	1	–	–	–	–	1
Yugoslavia	–	–	1	–	–	–	–	1
Czechoslovakia	–	–	–	–	1	–	–	1
Ireland	–	–	–	–	–	–	1	1
Taiwan	–	–	–	–	1	–	1	1
Total	41	97	120	9	166	95	68	595

Source: Jeffrey S. Arpan and David A. Ricks, eds., *Directory of Foreign Manufacturers in the United States,* 2nd ed. (Atlanta: Georgia State University, 1979).

historic regional employers such as textiles, apparel, and lumber. This is not to minimize the continued impact of these traditional southern industries, for textiles and apparel are projected to remain the region's largest employers through the late 1980s.

Whether the Southeast is able to take full advantage of the growth in employment projected for the emerging technology industries depends largely on how well it responds to the need to upgrade the skill levels of the work force. Only a renewed commitment to quality education and training programs can assure the region's ability to progress.

Service-type industries (such as transportation, communications, and public utilities; wholesale and retail trade; as well as finance, insurance, and real estate) will continue to grow in relative importance and will be the fastest growing categories of employment. While they currently provide about one-half of all nonfarm jobs, it is forecast that they will account for two-thirds of the future increases in jobs. Included in this category are such fast-growing areas as medical, child-care, business consulting, computer and systems consulting, information, and recreational and entertainment services.

The Southeast appears to be beyond the takeoff point for sustained economic growth. Further diversification in its economy should continue through the 1980s. However, the Southeast must avoid the mistakes made by many northern states. The region must continue to protect its business climate; develop and encourage programs of assistance to existing industry and small business; encourage the location of capital-intensive, advanced technology industry; provide upgraded technical and vocational training programs; introduce and refine the use of the computer and advanced communications as partial answers to educational deficiencies; and continue to encourage the location of foreign-owned manufacturing facilities.

If these things can be accomplished, the region will emerge as the realization of Henry Grady's dream of a "New South," whose economy has matured, and as a result of its own industrial revolution, can offer all its citizens the quality of life they deserve.

CHAPTER FOUR

Human Resource Utilization in the Southeast: An Examination of Racial Differences

GRETCHEN E. MACLACHLAN
Southern Center for Studies in Public Policy,
Clark College

Introduction

No forum devoted to exploring the critical issues relating to employment in the Southeast, and in my case to exploring human resource issues, can ignore the peculiar history of the southern region.[1] The South, unlike other regions, has had a past to live down. Slavery and the plantation agricultural economy were eliminated long ago, but their remnants have lingered on. The South has been more agricultural and rural, has had a larger black population, and has been poorer than other regions. Human resource development and utilization thus have been different in the South than elsewhere. Indeed, the South has changed, but two major questions remain: Has the South lost its unique characteristics and become indistinguishable from other regions? Has the subordination of the black population in the South ended?

In order to examine these two questions from the standpoint of human resource utilization, several variables describing the nature of the labor market experience of southern black and white workers and their economic consequences will be examined. Labor market experience variables will include labor force participation, unemployment, employment, and underemployment. Economic consequence variables will include earnings and poverty. To the extent available, trend data as well as current cross-sectional data are presented. Throughout this discussion, the two themes are the position of the region compared to the nation and the position of blacks compared to whites. A section on the region's population and educational development precedes the analysis of labor market experience and consequences.

Human Resources of the Southeast

The eight states of the southeastern region had a population of 38.9 million in 1980, of which 7.9 million were black.[2] Thus blacks comprised about one-fifth of the southeastern population, a proportion almost twice as high as the national percentage (11.7 percent) of blacks and slightly higher than that of the census South region (18.6 percent).[3] The proportion of blacks in the South has historically been declining, primarily because of their migration from the region but also because of the large-scale immigration of whites into the region.[4]

This century-old redistribution of the black population from the South to other regions, which has been especially heavy since World War II, has finally been arrested. Between 1975 and 1980 the migration of blacks into the South was greater than the out-migration of blacks.[5] Thus, a major social upheaval has subsided. The cessation of massive out-migration of blacks signifies a moderating of conditions for human resources at home compared to elsewhere.

Though interregional population redistribution has been stemmed for blacks, a redistribution within the South continues for both blacks and whites. The southern population is now more concentrated in urban and metropolitan areas than in the past, but the region is still less urbanized than are other regions. However, it is the only region in which population growth in the seventies in metropolitan areas was stronger than in nonmetropolitan areas; this growth has been greatest in small and medium-sized metropolitan areas.[6]

The black population in the South is more concentrated in metropolitan areas than is the southern white population; within metropolitan areas, blacks are more concentrated in central cities than are whites, who live predominantly in suburban areas (Exhibit 1). But the concentration of blacks in southern central cities is less pronounced than in other regions because proportionately more southern blacks are rural or nonmetropolitan residents than are blacks in other regions. However, the national pattern of pre-

Exhibit 1: **Residence of the Population, One Year and Older, in the South and United States**

	South		United States	
Area	Black	White	Black	White
Metropolitan	61.0%	54.5%	77.5%	65.9%
Central cities	41.8	21.4	56.6	23.3
Outside central cities	19.1	33.1	20.9	42.6
Nonmetropolitan	39.0	45.5	22.5	34.1
Total	100.0%	100.0%	100.0%	100.0%
Numbers in millions	11.47	59.42	25.86	190.19

Source: Computed from U.S. Bureau of the Census, Current Population Reports, Series P-20, No. 377, *Geographical Mobility: March 1980 to March 1981* (Washington, D.C.: Government Printing Office, 1983), Table 2, 8.

dominantly black central cities and white suburbs is being repeated since most job growth and new opportunities are not in central cities. The virtual segregation of the population racially will be an issue for the institutions that develop human resources.

Education

Although historically the educational development of the South's population has lagged behind that of the U.S. population, the region is catching up. The proportion of all persons 16 to 34 years old enrolled in school in 1979 was the same for the South as for the United States (50.2 and 50.3 percent, respectively); however, the enrollment rate for blacks was lower in the South (53.3, South; 55, United States).[7] But among some cohorts of the population, a higher proportion of blacks than of whites were enrolled in schools. High school completion among the southern population, however, is still behind that of the nation for whites and blacks (Exhibit 2), but the regional differential is much greater for blacks. The proportion of southern blacks who have completed high school is much lower than the proportion of whites in the South and of blacks nationally.

Because so many older blacks did not complete high school, these completion percentages will continue to lag behind the enrollment percentages for many decades. Among younger age groups, the discrepancy will be less extreme. Nevertheless, the ever-increasing tendency to require a high school diploma for employment places older southern blacks at a disadvantage.

Human Resource Utilization

This analysis of the utilization of the region's human resources is patterned after a study underway at the Southern Center for Studies in Public Policy, which is investigating the labor market status of blacks compared to whites nationwide over the past two decades.[8] Since our primary concern is the equality of blacks, the analytical scheme in both studies compares the races for each sex. To facilitate

Exhibit 2: **Percentage of High School Completions Among Persons, Twenty-five Years and Older, 1979**

	Black	White	Total
United States	49.4%	69.7%	67.7%
South	42.2	66.2	62.5

Source: U.S. Bureau of Census, Current Population Reports, Series P-20, No. 356, Educational Attainment in the United States: March 1979 and 1978 (Washington, D.C.: Government Printing Office, 1980), Table 7, 48-49.

these comparisons, black to white ratios are computed for all variables in order to assess the recent position and progress of blacks compared to whites.

For the first three variables discussed, a time series is available from 1974, the earliest year for which regional data by race were attainable. These data are annual averages compiled by the U.S. Bureau of Labor Statistics (BLS) from the monthly Current Population Survey. For regional trends BLS data is only available for "blacks and other races," referred to as nonwhites in this paper for convenience. Within the Southeast this poses no problem since the "other races" are a very small proportion of the total.[9] Labor market participation, employment, and unemployment will be described for men, followed by the same indicators for women.

Labor Market Indicators—Men

The labor force participation rate of nonwhite males in the Southeast declined steadily during the seventies (Exhibit 3). In 1974, the participation rate was four points higher (73.3 percent) than in 1981 (69.3 percent). In 1981, the labor force participation rate of white men in the region exceeded that of nonwhite men by about five points. The labor force participation among white men in the region declined, but slightly more slowly than for nonwhite men, declining by about three points since 1974.

These regional statistics on labor force participation rates and their trends do not depart substantially from the national pattern. Among nonwhite men, the national participation rate in 1981 (69.7 percent) was equivalent to that in the Southeast. The rates for nonwhite men in the Southeast and in the nation were virtually identical between 1974 and 1981. The rate of decline in nonwhite labor force participation rates was also about the same. In contrast, among white males nationally, the labor force participation rate in 1981 (77.9 percent) was about four points higher than the participation rate for white males in the Southeast. The presence of many retired white males in Florida skews the southeastern participation rate downward. Without Florida, the southeastern white male rate (calculated at 77.4 percent) was close to the 1981 U.S. rate. The opposite effect occurs among black men—excluding Florida depresses their southeastern participation rate.

Exhibit 3: **Males Sixteen Years and Older, Labor Force Participation, Employment/Population, and Unemployment Rates by Race, 1974-1981**

	1974	1975	1976	1977	1978	1979	1980	1981
Civilian Labor Force Participation Rate								
Southeast:								
Nonwhite	73.3	70.4	70.9	71.1	71.5	71.1	70.0	69.3
White	77.8	77.4	76.3	76.3	76.0	75.6	74.9	74.6
Nonwhite/White	.94	.91	.93	.93	.94	.94	.93	.93
United States:								
Nonwhite	73.3	71.5	70.7	71.0	72.1	71.9	70.8	69.7
White	79.4	78.7	78.4	78.5	78.6	78.6	78.3	77.9
Nonwhite/White	.92	.91	.90	.90	.92	.91	.90	.90
Employment to Population Ratio								
Southeast:								
Nonwhite	67.5	60.6	63.2	63.7	65.8	65.5	61.9	59.7
White	75.0	71.9	72.4	72.7	73.1	72.9	71.1	70.4
Nonwhite/White	.90	.84	.87	.88	.90	.90	.87	.85
United States:								
Nonwhite	66.6	61.7	61.7	62.3	64.2	64.5	61.4	59.9
White	76.0	73.0	73.4	74.2	75.1	75.1	73.5	72.9
Nonwhite/White	.88	.84	.84	.84	.85	.86	.84	.82
Unemployment Rate								
Southeast:								
Nonwhite	7.9	13.9	10.9	10.4	8.0	7.8	11.5	13.9
White	3.5	6.7	5.2	4.7	3.8	3.7	5.2	5.6
Nonwhite/White	2.26	2.07	2.10	2.21	2.11	2.11	2.21	2.48
United States:								
Nonwhite	9.2	13.6	12.7	12.3	11.0	10.4	13.2	14.1
White	4.4	7.2	6.4	5.5	4.6	4.5	6.1	6.5
Nonwhite/White	2.09	1.89	1.98	2.24	2.39	2.31	2.16	2.17

Source: Computed from U.S. Department of Labor, Bureau of Labor Statistics, *Geographic Profile of Employment and Unemployment, 1980*, Bulletin 2111; *Geographic Profile of Employment and Unemployment, 1981*, Bulletin 2156; *Employment Trends in the Southeast: 1974-1978*, Regional Report 53, (Washington, D.C.: Government Printing Office, 1980).

Throughout the period under examination, the participation rate among southeastern white men was lower than among their national couterparts. And the decline in these rates was faster in the Southeast than nationally, partially reflecting the growth of the retired population in Florida.

The relationship of the participation rates of nonwhite to white males in the Southeast remained close to the current ratio (.93) over the period. This compared favorably with the national ratio of .90, which also remained steady over the period. Thus, according to this indicator, black males have fared better compared to white males in the Southeast than in the entire United States.

The 1981 annual average unemployment rate for nonwhite men in the Southeast (13.9 percent) was barely below the national rate for nonwhite men (14.1 percent). In contrast, the unemployment rate for white men in the Southeast (5.6 percent) was about one point below the rate for white men nationally (6.5 percent). As a region, the South has historically had lower unemployment than other regions. During the eight years 1974–1981, the unemployment rate for nonwhite men in the region exceeded the national rate for nonwhite men only in 1975 (13.9 percent to 13.6 percent), and this difference is probably not statistically significant. In no year was the southeastern unemployment rate for white men above that for white men nationally.

Within the region the inferior position of blacks persists. In 1981 the nonwhite-to-white ratio of unemployment rates in the Southeast stood at a very high 2.48. This is more disparate than the ratio in the United States (2.17). The relative disadvantage of black male workers in the Southeast was greater in 1981 than in earlier recession years. This suggests not only a cyclical effect but also a long-term deterioration of the unemployment rate for southeastern black men compared to white men.

Though the complement of the unemployment rate is the employment rate, this is an insufficient statistic for fully measuring employment. Since the labor force concept requires active job-seeking status, many in the population without work are omitted. Thus not only will "not working or unemployment" be understated, but "working or employment" will be overstated. Minorities are more subject to this effect since more of them, relatively, are discouraged workers and other nonworkers who would accept jobs. A remedy is to use the employment-to-population ratio (E/P), which expresses employment as a percentage of the population sixteen years and older. The E/P has an advantage over the labor force participation rate for time series analysis because it reflects cyclical patterns, though it does so in more delayed fashion than unemployment rates.[10]

The employment-to-population ratio for the nonwhite male population in the Southeast declined precipitously from 1974 to 1981. The decline of nearly eight points in as many years represents a percentage decrease of 11.6 percent. Among white men in the region, the employment-to-population ratio declined nearly half as slowly as the decline for nonwhite men (6.1 percent). The ratio of nonwhite-to-white E/P ratios in 1974 was .90 but had declined substantially in 1975 (.84), since the employment of nonwhites was more affected than that of whites by the 1975 recession. The ratio of employment percentages gradually improved in the late seventies but then declined as another recession took a greater toll on nonwhites than on whites in the Southeast.

The employment-to-population ratio of nonwhite men nationwide was similar to that in the Southeast in 1981, and the decline from the percentage in 1974 was similar as well. The percentage of the U.S. white male population employed in 1981 was higher than in the Southeast—72.9 percent compared to 76.0 percent. This gap had increased since 1974, when the national rate was only one percentage point higher.

Comparing the national ratios for nonwhite men to white men shows the disparity in the position of minorities. The ratio between nonwhite and white men of their employment-to-population ratios was only .82 in 1981, having fallen six points in eight years with the same pattern of falls and rises as in the Southeast. Thus a major deterioration in the employment of nonwhites occurred nationally as well as regionally. Though the recessions of 1975 and 1980 had a more severe effect on minorities, economic upturns did not return them to prerecession levels because structural deterioration occurred.

Labor Market Indicators—Women

In contrast to male labor market indicators, those for the female labor force show less difference regionally and between the races. The rising trend in the labor force participation of women was marked for both nonwhite and white women in the Southeast and in the United States from 1974 to 1981. The labor force participation rate for nonwhite women in the region increased by 8.4 percent, rising from 50 percent to 54.2 percent (Exhibit 4). The increase in labor force participation of white women in the Southeast was slightly greater, in excess of 9 percent, but their 1981 participation rate was still lower than the rate for nonwhite women.

The participation rate for nonwhite women in the nation as a whole increased at a similar rate to that in the Southeast. However, the rise in the labor force participation for white women nationally was even sharper than the rise among nonwhite women nationally and among southern women, nonwhite or white. The participation rate for U.S. white women grew by 15 percent from 1974 to 1981.

How do recent trends compare with the past? The labor force participation rate for women has been higher outside the South than in the South in recent decades. It has also been higher among nonwhite women than among white women. The experience of the years 1974 to 1981 shows that the regional differential virtually disappeared for nonwhite women. However, for white women, the parity in labor force participation that existed in 1974 between southeastern and national rates has dissolved. The 1981 differential (2.5 percent) in rates of participation of white women between the Southeast and the United States is similar to the differential in 1960 (2 percent) for the South and the United States.[11]

The racial differential in labor force participation rates for women is greater in the Southeast than nationally. But these ratios of the nonwhite-to-white rates in the United States and the Southeast are less disparate than in the more distant past, because white female labor force participation has risen so dramatically in the last

Exhibit 4: **Females Sixteen Years and Older, Labor Force Participation, Employment/Population, and Unemployment Rates by Race, 1974–1981**

	1974	1975	1976	1977	1978	1979	1980	1981
Civilian Labor Force Participation Rate								
Southeast:								
Nonwhite	50.0	50.0	51.5	51.0	52.7	51.7	52.7	54.2
White	45.3	45.5	46.2	47.3	48.2	48.6	49.2	49.5
Nonwhite/White	1.10	1.10	1.11	1.08	1.09	1.06	1.07	1.09
United States:								
Nonwhite	49.1	49.2	50.2	50.9	53.3	53.5	53.4	53.4
White	45.2	45.9	48.9	48.1	49.5	50.6	51.3	52.0
Nonwhite/White	1.09	1.07	1.03	1.06	1.08	1.06	1.04	1.03
Employment to Population Ratio								
Southeast:								
Nonwhite	44.5	42.3	44.1	43.5	45.3	44.7	45.2	45.8
White	42.7	41.6	43.1	44.2	45.4	45.8	46.1	46.2
Nonwhite/White	1.04	1.02	1.02	.98	1.00	.98	.98	.99
United States:								
Nonwhite	43.8	42.3	43.3	43.8	46.4	46.9	46.4	45.8
White	42.4	42.0	43.2	44.6	46.4	47.6	48.0	48.4
Nonwhite/White	1.03	1.01	1.00	.98	1.00	.99	.97	.95
Unemployment Rate								
Southeast:								
Nonwhite	11.2	15.5	14.3	14.7	14.0	13.5	14.4	15.3
White	5.6	8.5	6.8	6.6	5.7	5.6	6.2	6.6
Nonwhite/White	2.00	1.82	2.10	2.23	2.46	2.41	2.32	2.33
United States:								
Nonwhite	10.8	13.9	13.6	13.9	13.0	12.3	13.1	14.3
White	6.1	8.6	7.9	7.3	6.2	5.9	6.5	6.9
Nonwhite/White	1.77	1.62	1.72	1.90	2.17	2.08	2.02	2.07

Source: Computed from U.S. Department of Labor, Bureau of Labor Statistics, *Geographic Profile of Employment and Unemployment, 1980*, Bulletin 2111; *Geographic Profile of Employment and Unemployment, 1981*, Bulletin 2156; *Employment Trends in the Southeast: 1974–1978*, Regional Report 53, (Washington, D.C.: Government Printing Office, 1980).

three decades. And while the participation rate of white women nationally is still below that of nonwhite women, their rates are converging. In the Southeast the ratio of the nonwhite female participation rate to the white female rate was 1.09. With the exception of 1979 and 1980, the nonwhite-to-white ratio was about 1.09 to 1.11 over the years 1974-1981. For the nation, the ratio between the participation of nonwhite and white women in 1981 was closer to parity than the ratio for the Southeast—1.03.

The unemployment rate trends for women regionally and nationally show opposite effects for minority and white women Among nonwhite women the unemployment rate regionally was higher than for the nation (15.3 to 14.3 percent) in 1981 and was throughout the eight-year period. The peak rate was during the 1975 recession, but the 1981 rate was nearly as high. On the other hand, the unemployment rate of southern white women in 1981 was lower than nationally (6.6 to 6.9 percent) and was throughout the eight years.

The racial differentials in unemployment rates for women are similar to those discussed for men. The ratios deteriorated regionally (from 2.00 to 2.33) and nationally (from 1.77 to 2.07), and the regional ratios were consistently above national ones. Thus, the unemployment burden has grown relatively more for southeastern black women compared to white women in the Southeast and black women in the nation.

The employment percentages for white women in the Southeast and in the United States continued their robust upward growth during the period under examination. In contrast, the trend for nonwhite women nationally and regionally was interrupted by frequent cyclical downturns in their employment percentage. Among southeastern nonwhite women, the ratio of employment to population stood at 45.8 percent in 1981, which was the highest point over the eight years. But the rate fluctuated, declining in 1975, 1977, and 1979. Among white women in the region, the employment-to-population ratio was also at its highest point (46.2 percent). The rate declined in 1975, but in no other year during the eight-year period. For white women nationally, the employment-to-population ratio was at its highest point (48.4 percent) in 1981. But for nonwhite women, it was below its 1979 high and was 45.6 percent in 1981.

Regional differences in the employment-to-population ratios are minimal. Nonwhite women in the Southeast and in the United States had similar rates of employment over the eight years. The percentage of white women employed nationally in 1981 was two points higher than in the Southeast, growing from near equivalence in 1974.

Racial disparities in the labor force participation of nonwhite and white women appear to be reversing nationally and in the Southeast. Between 1979 and 1981, the ratio of the employment percentage for nonwhite women to white women fell below parity. In earlier years, a higher proportion of nonwhite women were employed compared to white women. Thus, the disparity reversed from a higher employment percentage for nonwhites compared to whites to a higher percentage of whites compared to nonwhites.

In summary, the labor market indicators for men and women of both races are similar in the region and nation. For labor force participation, the position of southeastern men and women is similar to their counterparts nationally. The unemployment rate shows a better relative position of southeastern workers compared to workers nationally, except for nonwhite women. The employment-to-population ratios show little difference between regional and national counterparts.

The relationship between the races shows relative deterioration in the Southeast compared to the United States for nonwhite men and women, as measured by the ratios of the unemployment rates and the employment-to-population ratios. There was no relative deterioration between minorities and whites in their participation in the work force. But there was a substantial deterioration in the utilization of nonwhites and whites. The employment gap between nonwhite and white men has soared in the region and the nation. Among women the traditionally greater employment of nonwhites has been reversed. The disparity in unemployment between nonwhites and whites is rising nationally and regionally.

Underemployment Indicators

In 1982 the U.S. Commission on Civil Rights issued a report on the unemployment and underemployment among blacks, women, and Hispanics.[12] Region was among the factors that were investigated for their effects on the labor market situation of minorities and women compared to majority males. Examining 1980 Current Population Survey data, the commission used several indicators to measure underemployment, including intermittent employment, involuntary part-time employment, marginal jobs, and workers in poverty households. The commission's findings for the various groups according to region will be discussed for each indicator (see summary Exhibit 5). Ratios were computed between the races (black males to white males and black females to white females). The demographic categories used by the commission exclude white Hispanics from the "white" category and other racial minorities so that the "black" category is blacks only. This is the best scheme for analyzing racial disparities. The regional categories used are those of the Census Bureau.

Intermittent employment—unemployment of at least fifteen weeks or at least three separate spells of unemployment during a year—is less of a problem for whites in the South than in other regions. For white men and women the percentages of intermittent employment were lower in the South than in any other region (4.6 and 3.3 percent repectively). For blacks, the South neither registered the lowest nor the highest regional percentages of the intermittently employed. The percentages for southern blacks were 11.2 percent for males and 7.8 percent for females. For black male workers intermittent employment was most severe in the West (15.7 percent), and for black women workers, in the North Central region (9.5 percent). Though the South does not have the highest incidence of intermittent employment among regions, it has the greatest inequality between the races in the percentage of intermittent employment. Black women in the South are about 2.36 times as likely as white women to be affected by intermittent employment; black men, 2.43 times as likely as white men. For men, the ratio is greater in the West, where black men are 2.66 times as likely as white men to be intermittently employed.

The incidence of involuntary part-time employment was more severe for blacks in the South than in any other region and comparatively low among white workers in the South. In 1980, 6 percent of southern black men and 7 percent of southern black women were employed part-time due to economic circumstances. Only 2.5 percent of white men and 3.4 percent of white women were

Exhibit 5: **Percentages of Underemployment by Race, Sex, and Region of Residence, and Black to White Ratios of Underemployment, March 1980**

Region	Males			Females		
	Black	White	B/W Ratios	Black	White	B/W Ratios
Intermittently Employed						
South	11.2%	4.6%	2.42	7.8%	3.3%	2.36
Northeast	11.1	5.4	2.06	6.8	4.7	1.45
North Central	10.4	5.6	1.87	9.5	4.1	2.32
West	15.7	5.9	2.66	9.1	4.1	2.22
Total	11.5	5.3	2.16	8.1	4.0	2.02
Involuntary Part Time						
South	6.0	2.5	2.39	7.0	3.4	2.06
Northeast	4.3	2.4	1.81	4.8	4.0	1.20
North Central	2.9	2.9	1.00	5.9	3.7	1.59
West	5.2	3.1	1.69	4.2	3.4	1.24
Total	5.0	2.7	1.84	6.1	3.6	1.69
Marginal Jobs						
South	12.1	4.5	2.67	26.7	12.7	2.10
Northeast	12.3	6.5	1.90	17.0	13.8	1.23
North Central	12.4	5.5	2.25	16.8	15.4	1.09
West	8.5	4.6	1.86	14.2	13.1	1.08
Total	11.9	5.3	2.25	21.7	13.9	1.56
Workers in Poverty Households						
South	6.2	2.8	2.24	8.8	2.1	4.19
Northeast	2.2	1.3	1.71	3.6	1.6	2.25
North Central	2.3	2.0	1.12	5.4	1.5	3.60
West	4.5	2.0	2.29	3.6	1.9	1.89
Total	4.5	2.1	2.18	6.6	1.8	3.67

Source: U.S. Commission on Civil Rights, *Unemployment and Underemployment Among Blacks, Hispanics, and Women*, Clearinghouse Publication 74 (November 1982), Table 4.2 for percentages; Appendix B, section 2–5 for ratios of Black to White for Males; ratios of Black to White for Females were computed.

similarly affected. The resulting racial disparity was 2.4 for men and about 2.0 for women, both the highest for any region.

A third variable for measuring underemployment in the commission's study was marginal jobs. These are jobs that require three months or less of specific vocational training. The percentage of black women holding marginal jobs was greatest in the South, where more than one-fourth (26.7 percent) of the region's black women held such employment. About the same percentage, 12 percent, of black men in the South as in two other regions (the North Central and Northeast) held marginal jobs. In contrast, the percentage of white men and women in marginal jobs was lower in the South than in other regions. Only 4.5 percent of southern white men held marginal jobs, as did 12.7 percent of southern white women. The disparities in the ratio of black to white percentages holding marginal jobs was highest in the South for both men and women. For southern men, the black rate was 2.7 times the white rate. For southern women, the percentage of blacks holding marginal jobs was more than twice that for whites.

The fourth underemployment variable measured family poverty among workers. If a worker was employed at least one month during the year and the family income was below the poverty line, the individual was classified as a worker in a poverty household. The South had a higher incidence of working poor, according to this measurement, for all four of the demographic groups, but the incidence was much higher for black than for white workers. The percentage of workers in a poverty family was 8.8 percent of black women, 6.2 percent of black men, 2.8 percent of white men, and 2.1 percent of white women. The ratio of racial disparity between southern black and white women was 4.19, the highest of any region. Among men it was 2.2, just below the ratio for the West.

Of these four indicators of underemployment, all except intermittent employment were more severe problems in the South than in other regions for black workers. The incidence of involuntary part-time employment was highest in the South for black men and women. The incidence of workers in poverty households was also highest in the South for black men and women. For black women, the percentage in marginal jobs was much higher in the South compared to other regions. For whites, only one underemployment measure was more severe in the South than in other regions—the percentage of workers in poverty families. But two other indicators show lower underemployment for whites in the South compared to other regions; these are marginal jobs and intermittent employment. Except for the poverty of workers measure, underemployment in the South is much more a black than a white phenomenon.

Consequently, the racial disparities between blacks and whites within regions are greatest in the South. Black women are more disadvantaged, according to all four underemployment measures, and black men are more disadvantaged, according to two indicators (involuntary part-time and marginal jobs). Also, the South is virtually tied with the West as the most inequitable region according to the poverty workers measure.

Earnings Rates

The earnings of southern workers have lagged behind the rest of the United States, and blacks in the South have lagged behind whites. Has this changed in the latest "New South"? Greater underemployment in the South, particularly among blacks, results in lower annual earnings for blacks compared to whites. But are fully employed southerners more poorly paid than nonsoutherners, and blacks than whites? One series that eliminates the effect of unemployment and underemployment is the usual weekly earnings series of the Bureau of Labor Statistics. This report provides the median usual weekly earnings rate for full-time wage and salary workers. It allows a comparison of weekly earnings rates between regions and races for each sex.

In 1982, the median usual weekly rate of earnings for black men in the South was the lowest of all regions ($246 compared to $281 for the United States)[13] Similarly, white men in the South registered a median earning rate below that for all regions ($351 compared to $382).[14] But white southern men are closer to their national counterparts than southern black men to all black men nationwide in terms of earnings rates (Exhibit 6). The ratio of the southern median to the U.S. median shows that white southern men earn .92 of white men nationally and black men earn, .88 of black men nationally. Thus, the South is still behind the rest of the nation.

Exhibit 6: **Ratios of Median Usual Weekly Earnings for Full-Time Wage and Salary Workers, Between Nonwhites or Blacks to Whites by Sex and Region and South to United States by Race and by Sex, 1973 to 1982***

	'73	'74	'75	'76	'77	'78	'79	'80	'81	'82
Nonwhite or Black to White					**Males**					
United States	.77	.77	.77	.79	.78	.78	.76	.75	.76	.74
South	.68	70	.60	.00	.70	.69	.71	.72	.71	.70
Northeast	.83	.86	.87	.86	.87	.87	.83	.78	.82	.78
North Central	.85	.84	.91	.95	.92	.87	.89	.91	.90	.87
West	.88	.91	.89	.89	.92	.91	.85	.85	.84	.82
South/United States										
Nonwhite or Black	.79	.83	.84	.81	.82	.81	.87	.89	.87	.88
White	.90	.91	.93	.93	.92	.91	.93	94	.93	.92
Nonwhite or Black to White					**Females**					
United States	.91	.94	.94	.93	.93	.94	.93	.92	.93	.91
South	.83	.87	.85	.90	.86	.87	.86	.89	.88	.86
Northeast	1.05	1.04	1.03	1.03	1.00	1.03	1.01	1.00	.99	.99
North Central	1.03	.96	1.11	1.05	1.04	1.07	1.02	1.00	1.03	1.01
West	.99	1.00	1.01	.96	1.00	1.04	1.02	.99	1.01	1.05
South/United States										
Nonwhite or Black	.83	.85	.82	.88	.86	.87	.87	.90	.89	.88
White	.90	.92	.91	.92	.93	.94	.94	.94	.94	.94

Source: U.S. Department of Labor, Bureau of Labor Statistics, unpublished tabulations from the Current Population Survey, annual averages since 1979, May data prior to 1979.

*Data for 1973 to 1978 are for nonwhites; for 1979 to 1982, for blacks only.

However, progress was made over the past decade for black men. In 1973, the ratio of the median usual weekly earnings for the South compared to the nation was .79. The ratio rose to a high point of .89 in 1979, a ten-point improvement. But in the last two years the ratio has dropped. Thus, the gain of southern black men appears to have leveled off. Only a modest gain of about .02 was made by southern white men compared to white men nationally.

While the relative standing of southern men, both black and white, improved, the position of black men compared to white men showed less movement toward equality. The data suggest that racial inequality, which has typified the South, is increasing in other regions while decreasing slightly in the South. The ten-year trend in the racial parity ratio (of black male earnings to white male earnings) in the South showed improvement from 1973 to 1980, but has dropped since then. In three regions, however, the disparity between the races grew more pronounced. In the Northeast the ratio of black to white median earnings was .78, having decreased from .83 in just three years. In the North Central a decline occurred after near parity between nonwhites and whites in 1976 (.95). The West is a special case. Prior to 1979 the data series combined "other races" with blacks but now is for blacks only. Before the change in the racial categories, the nonwhite to white ratio increased to a high point in 1977. After the change in 1979, the black-to-white ratio was .05 lower than the preceding year because of the exclusion of other races (mostly Orientals), whose earnings are higher than blacks' earnings in the West. The four years of black-only data for the West show the same decrease as other regions in the racial parity ratio.

These ratios signify a growing racial inequality in regions outside the South. The four regions appear to be moving toward convergence in terms of racial inequities in median usual earnings. The slight improvement for black men relative to white men in the South has been matched by deterioration in equality of earnings between the races in other regions.

In contrast to men's earning relationships, there is less racial disparity between black and white women, but in the southern region a differential exists. In 1982, the median for black women in the South was $197 and for white women $230; both figures are the lowest for all regions.[15] The ratio between them (.86) is the most disparate among regions. In two of the other three regions (West and North Central), black women earn more than white women. Over the past ten years the ratio of black (or nonwhite) to white earnings has changed little. The ratios increased slightly in the South and in the West. In the Northeast the ratio decreased from parity to below parity. In the North Central the ratio fluctuated but in 1982 was about the same as ten years previously—at parity. As in the case of the men, the median usual earnings of southern women, compared to their national counterparts, has improved, more so for black than white women.

Poverty

While the foregoing earnings analysis charts the progress of full-time workers, the analysis of the South's position is incomplete. It needs to be augmented by a final set of data that examines the extent of poverty (Exhibit 7). The long-standing poverty of the South has been a hallmark of the region, as has been the disproportionate burden of the region's poverty on its black population. The social programs of the past two decades and the improvements in the position of black workers have had a salutary effect on the region's black poor. The incidence of poverty has declined for blacks. In 1980, 35 percent of blacks in the South were in poverty in contrast to 43 percent ten years earlier. Most of the improvement occurred in the first half of the seventies when the black poverty rate declined by six percentage points. Among southern whites, the percentage in poverty was essentially the same in 1980 as in 1970—12 percent.

The improvement in the poverty situation among southern blacks has resulted in a decrease in the ratio of the black to white poverty percentages. The ratio has declined from 3.4 in 1970 to 2.9 in 1980. This improvement should not obscure the fact that in excess of one-third of all southern blacks are still poor.

In the remainder of the United States, poverty among blacks has been multiplying. In the non-South regions the incidence of poverty among blacks in 1970 was 19 percent, but in 1980 it was nearly 30 percent. The increase has been most pronounced in the Northeast where nearly 31 percent of blacks are now poor, an increase of 11 points over 1970. In the North Central region the percentage of blacks in poverty rose from 26 to 33 percent and in the East the percentage rose in the mid-seventies but declined to 19 percent in 1980, about the same rate as ten years earlier.

The effect of these changes on the incidence of black poverty regionally has been to alter the regional poverty differential almost

Exhibit 7: **Percentage of Persons Below the Poverty Level and Ratios of Poverty by Race and Region, 1970, 1975, and 1980**

	1970	1975	1980
Blacks	Percentage Below the Poverty Level		
United States	33.1%	31.3%	32.5%
South	42.6%	36.6%	35.1%
Non-South	19.1%	25.2%	29.6%
Northeast	20.0%	24.5%	30.7%
North Central	25.7	25.5	33.3
West	20.4	26.2	19.0
Whites			
United States	9.9%	9.7%	10.2%
South	12.4%	11.4%	12.2%
Non-South	8.9%	9.0%	9.3%
Northeast	7.6%	8.8%	8.9%
North Central	8.9	8.1	8.9
West	10.6	10.6	10.4
Black/White Ratio	Ratios of Poverty Percentages		
United States	3.34%	3.25%	3.19%
South	3.44%	3.21%	2.88%
Non-South	2.15%	2.80%	3.18%
Northeast	2.63%	2.78%	3.45%
North Central	2.89	3.15	3.74
West	1.92	2.47	1.83
South/Non-South Ratio			
Blacks	2.23%	1.45%	1.19%
Whites	1.39	1.27	1.31

Source: Percentages from U.S. Bureau of the Census, Current Population Reports, Series P-60, No. 133, *Characteristics of the Population Below the Poverty Level: 1980*; ratios were computed.

to the point of parity. In 1970 the percentage of poverty in the South was 2.23 times the percentage in the non-South regions. In 1980, however, the percentage in the South was only 1.19 of that in the non-South. Thus, the regions are converging, and the perennial differential of regional southern poverty for blacks is disappearing. Were the convergence from high rates to lower rates in all regions, the trend would be welcomed. But the change amounts to a redistribution of the nation's black poor. The national incidence of poverty among black persons is almost 33 percent, unchanged from a decade earlier.

Among whites in regions outside the South, the percentage in poverty has remained virtually constant in all regions over the ten years, at about 9 percent. The incidence of poverty among southern whites was unchanged over the ten years, thus the South to non-South ratio of poverty percentages has remained similar (1.39 in 1970 and 1.31 in 1980).

Conclusion

Returning to the first of my two original questions: Has the South lost its unique characteristics and become indistinguishable from the rest of the United States? In terms of labor force participation and employment, black and white men in the Southeast are virtually identical to their national counterparts. This is becoming true for unemployment as well. Among women, within race there are also no striking differences between the Southeast and the United States for labor market participation, employment, and unemployment. However, underemployment in the South is not identical to the United States. Whites in the South are less subject to underemployment than whites in other regions, but blacks in the South are more subject to underemployment than blacks in other regions. In earnings, the South has been moving in the direction of parity with the United States, though it has not yet reached that goal. The regional poverty differential within races is also abating. The method of analysis used here, of separating the races and also the sexes for some variables, has made it possible to reach these conclusions. What have sometimes been construed as regional differences are, in fact, racial differences that have shown up as regional differences because of the concentration of about one-half of the nation's blacks in the Southeast region.

This brings me to my second question: Has the subordination of the black population in the South ended? The answer is no, rather it is being nationalized. Serious problems are no longer the lot primarily of southern blacks. Nationally and regionally there is an alarming level of non-employment among black men, both unemployment and lack of participation in the labor force. For black women nationally and in the South, there is high unemployment and underemployment. Earnings ratios between the races indicate a deterioration of black earnings compared to white earnings in regions outside the South. And poverty, which had been more of a southern problem, is now a problem for blacks nationally.

Do these conclusions imply that the Southeast need not concern itself with questions of equality? No. The region is home for more blacks than any other region and, indeed, is attracting more blacks. Thus attention must be directed toward these problems. The continuing health of the Sunbelt demands better conditions for its black population.

Endnotes

1. Mindful that this conference was directed to issues in the Southeast, to the extent possible, data pertain to the eight southeastern states for which the Bureau of Labor Statistics reports labor market statistics: North Carolina, South Carolina, Georgia, Florida, Alabama, Mississippi, Tennessee, and Kentucky. However, for other variables the sixteen-state census region South was used, which in addition to the above states includes Delaware, Maryland, Virginia, West Virginia, Louisiana, Arkansas, Texas, Oklahoma, and the District of Columbia.

2. Computed from U.S. Bureau of the Census, 1980 Census of Population, *Race of the Population by State: 1980*, Supplementary Report, PC 80-S1-3, Table 1, 6.

3. Ibid., Table 2, 8.

4. David H. Swinton, "Racial Inequality in the New South," unpublished manuscript, 1983.

5. U.S. Bureau of the Census, Current Population Reports, Series P-20, No. 368, *Geographical Mobility: March 1975 to March 1980* (Washington, D.C.: Government Printing Office, 1981), 1.

6. U.S. Bureau of the Census, Current Population Reports, Series P-20, Number 374, *Population Profile of the United States: 1981* (Washington, D.C.: Government Printing Office, 1982), Table 2-6, 13.

7. U.S. Bureau of the Census, Current Population Report, Series P-20, Number 360, *School Enrollment-Social and Economic Characteristics of Students: October 1979* (Washington, D.C.: Government Printing Office, 1980), Table 9, 26.

8. Southern Center for Studies in Public Policy, "The Labor Market Position of Black Americans: A State of the Art Assessment Over Two Decades, 1960–1980," unpublished manuscript, 1983

9. The national study uses unpublished data from the BLS reported for "blacks only." Incidentally, we have found that the combination of blacks and other races in the reporting of various statistics usually portrays the situation of blacks as better than it is. Regionally, this is a particular problem in the data for the West.

10. Carol Boyd Leon, "The Employment-Population Ratio: Its Value in Labor Force Analysis," *Monthly Labor Review* (February 1981): 38.

11. Historical data from James G. Maddox et al., *The Advancing South* (New York: The Twentieth Century Fund, 1967), Appendix Table 7-2, 256.

12. U.S. Commission on Civil Rights, *Unemployment and Underemployment Among Blacks, Hispanics, and Women*, Clearinghouse Publication 74 (November 1982).

13. U.S. Department of Labor, Bureau of Labor Statistics, unpublished data from the Current Population Survey, annual averages.

14. Ibid.

15. Ibid.

Personnel Issues
of the 1980s

DAVID MOORE

Chairman, Management Department,
University of North Florida

My assignment is to focus on personnel issues that I see as most pressing during the decade of the 1980s. Many of these issues will be carryovers from the past, particularly the recent past. It is useful, therefore, to begin our analysis with a review of the personnel issues of the decade just past and to relate current and emerging developments to them.

Issues of the 1970s

While I was still at The Conference Board in New York, Allen Janger of the board's division of management research completed a landmark study of the changing objectives and organization of the personnel function in business.[1] This study was based on a questionnaire survey covering 673 senior personnel executives, supplemented by interviews with more than 300 executives in over 100 companies. The main body of information represents the views of personnel executives in 1975 and 1976. The study, therefore, reflects the impact of new employment laws in the areas of equal employment opportunity, occupational safety and health, and employee retirement.

Equal Employment Opportunity and Changing Employment Policies

It is important to keep in mind that federal and state laws affecting employees have been major factors in shaping personnel activities at least since the 1930s. One has only to recall the National Labor Relations Act, the Fair Labor Standards Act, Walsh-Healy, and the myriad of state laws affecting employment to realize that the personnel function in industry is largely an extension of government. Accordingly, the laws affecting employment that were passed in the 1960s and 1970s were not wholly new incursions of the federal government into the affairs of personnel departments. The government had been there many times before, but with the exception of the National Labor Relations Act no previous law had so profound an effect on personnel practices as the Civil Rights Act of 1964.

Of particular importance was the Supreme Court decision in *Griggs v. Duke Power Company* that specifically dealt with employment requirements commonly used in industry, such as high school completion requirements and the ability to pass tests at a level arbitrarily set by the personnel department. The Supreme Court stated with reference to *Griggs*:

> On the record before us, neither the high school completion requirement nor the general intelligence test is shown to bear a demonstrable relationship to successful performance of the jobs for which it was used. Both were adopted...without meaningful study of their relationship to job-performance ability. Rather, a vice president of the Company testified, the requirements were instituted on the Company's judgment that they would generally improve the overall quality of the work force.[2]

The decision revolutionized the employment philosophy that prevailed in industry at that time. This philosophy mainly reflected the needs and interests of the company rather than those of the applicant. Previous to *Griggs v. Duke*, the personnel departments of most companies saw their task, as the Duke vice president testified, to be that of improving "the overall quality of the work force." No one up to that point had questioned the right of private employers to set their own standards of quality. Accordingly, the typical company overhired if possible, built up reservoirs of potentially promotable employees, and set standards that were appropriate for future positions but often irrelevant for jobs at hand. Some went even further than this, setting attitudinal, personal, and social standards in addition to educational and experiential requirements. The idea was that employees not only had to be able to do the job but also had to fit into an existing social structure. One major consulting firm urged employers to interview the wives of potential managers in order to answer questions like these:

Are the wife's ambitions and desires consistent with the social role called for by the job?

Is the type of relationship between the husband and wife one that will allow him to apply himself full time to his job?

According to this consultant, the ideal wife from the employer's point of view is "one who is free from major emotional maladjustments; regards marriage as a cooperative venture; and is willing to make whatever concessions and sacrifices may be necessary to sustain her end of the partnership."[3]

Such considerations as these seem almost archaic in the 1980s, not only because of changes in the law, but because of social changes as well. Yet, a few short years ago, they did not appear quite so outlandish. Most women stayed close to the hearth and saw their role as that of helpmate (freely translated as "wife") to their spouses, who were the principal breadwinners and primary mediators between the home and the outside world of work. Indeed, as recently as 1960, less than a third of even very young wives between the ages of 20 and 24 worked outside the home. Among the older wives, the percentage was much less. By 1980, most married women of all ages participated in the labor force. Among younger wives the percentage was twice what it was in 1960. Old patterns clearly were fast disappearing by the 1980s.

It is not at all surprising that two-thirds of the companies included in the Conference Board study of 1975-76 regarded equal employment opportunity as a "major" activity at the corporate level.[4] In fact, in over 50 percent of the board's sample companies, the company president "participated significantly in policy formulation" with respect to equal employment opportunity. Obviously, the concern at top levels resulted from something more than just a change in employment philosophy. That "something more" was financial risk. The AT&T consent agreement of 1973, which cost the company as much as $55 million, was enough to get top executives in even the giant corporations to sit up and take notice. The personnel function, as one executive put it, "became too important for the personnel staff to handle alone." However, top management attention had the effect of enhancing personnel activities. Moreover, all personnel transactions, including transfers and promotions as well as hiring, now had to be filtered through the personnel department's controls.

Centralization of Personnel Policy

The equal employment opportunity laws and regulations plus compliance activities related to the Occupational Safety and Health Act of 1970 (OSHA) and the Employee Retirement Income Security Act of 1974 (ERISA) all compelled centralization of personnel policymaking and control at the corporate level. In the two decades prior to the new employment laws, large companies had been decentralizing the personnel function to the divisions. Now, according to the Conference Board study, they were structuring the personnel function along the familiar organizational pattern of centralization of policy, planning, and control, and decentralization of implementation and routine administration.[5]

Staffing Systems and Human Resources Management

Other trends also were moving the personnel departments of the 1970s toward a closer relationship with top management. These trends were related to corporate management's growing concern with long-range planning and with the coordination of functional activities toward explicitly identified goals and objectives. Personnel departments, like the other functional departments, were caught up with these trends, which took the form of planning and developing staffing systems. Previously, manpower planning, if done at all, proceeded without particular reference to the long-range goals of the business. Indeed, the overall missions of major corporations seemed to change slowly enough to permit personnel departments to concentrate primarily on the *number* of employees that would be needed rather than the *types, skills, and abilities* that would be required. As the Conference Board study reports: "In the absence of corporate long-range planning, training or recruiting for future needs was a matter of guesswork. Many recruitment, training, and compensation units developed rules of thumb to estimate their workload, but typically their estimates were rarely shared and almost never coordinated."[6]

The new approach to systematic staffing covered almost every major personnel activity, including forecasting manpower needs, identifying recruiting sources, specifying job requirements and hiring criteria, setting management development objectives, determining training methods, developing training programs, designing jobs and organizational structures to facilitate overall objectives and accommodate staffing requirements, designing appropriate compensation and benefit packages, and negotiating necessary changes in the labor contract.

Because of its comprehensiveness and coordination with the overall goals of the enterprise, the staffing system approach appeared to answer some of the questions raised by Peter Drucker two decades before when he maintained that "personnel administration...is largely a collection of incidental techniques without much internal cohesion."[7] Indeed, staffing systems and strategies seemed to some of the senior personnel executives in the Conference Board study to provide a "major focus for managing the personnel function as a whole." As a result, a number began to call themselves "Vice President for Human Resources" to reflect this central, co-ordinating focus.

The expanding role of the personnel department in ensuring compliance with government employment laws and in planning and coordinating staffing activities resulted in a greatly enhanced interest in personnel management information systems in the mid-1970s. The computer made possible highly sophisticated analyses of the costs and effects of various personnel policies and programs.

It also permitted the coordination of vast quantities of personnel data in the development of complex planning models.

Organizational Development

I am sure that it won't surprise any of you to learn from the Conference Board study that many companies were engaged in organizational development activities in the 1970s, but what will surprise you is that no mention was made of Japanese management techniques in this connection. The popular interest in Japanese management methods is only a few years old and can be dated by the appearance of a plethora of articles and books on the subject from 1979 through 1981. Throughout the 1970s, however, there was a growing concern with the diminished growth of productivity in the United States that became very serious during the 1979–1982 period when there was practically no growth at all. However, before 1975, American management was still basking in the glow of the relatively successful 1960s. Interestingly, Jean Jacques Servan-Schreiber's book *The American Challenge*, in which he described U.S. corporations in Europe as being well on their way to becoming the third largest industrial power after the United States and USSR, was first published in 1967.[8] How times change! It took only a decade for American management to go from hero to bum. I wonder how long the Japanese star will be ascendant!

In any event, the interest of U.S. management in organizational development and behavioral techniques during this period was perhaps more related to the quality of work life than to productivity.[9] Personnel staffs were particularly interested in the changing composition of the work force and the increasing numbers of professionally and technically trained employees. There was also talk at this time about the malaise of blue-collar workers, particularly among automobile workers. Younger employees presumably were unwilling to accept the deadly boredom of the assembly line and were demanding greater say-so in their work. The strike at the Lordstown, Ohio, General Motors plant received much attention because it was presumably not over wages but rather over the dehumanizing nature of work on the assembly line. For these and other reasons, management became more extensively involved in job design, job rotation, decision making, employee attitude surveys and feedback, and other techniques in order to reduce monotony and improve the quality of work life. According to the Conference Board study, more than eight out of ten companies surveyed were involved with organizational development, which had become "among the fastest growing of the new activities and ... made the personnel staff a primary company employer of professional psychologists, sociologists, and an occasional cultural anthropologist."[10]

Other new emphases identified by personnel executives in the Conference Board study were, for example, the rising interest in employee training (in part related to the upgrading of minority employees) and the concern with employee compensation as a result of inflation. None of these other issues, however, compared with the concern with equal opportunity, the growing linkage and coordination of the personnel staffing function with top management planning, and the interest in quality of work life and organizational development, particularly as an outgrowth of the unrest that started on the campuses and spilled over into corporate offices and annual stockholder meetings. Note that these concerns all grew out of events that occurred during the late 1960s and early 1970s and represented management's adaptation to compelling changes in the business environment.

Issues of the 1980s

The problems of one decade do not abruptly end with the beginning of the next but rather merge with the new challenges that unfold. Human resource management is a never-ending process of building, developing, adapting, disbanding, and reconstituting organizations. The basic problems may remain the same, but the way they are dealt with will vary with the ebb and flow of organizational growth and decay. Thus, the issue of equal opportunity was essentially a hiring and promotion problem in the 1970s but became a problem of maintaining gains already achieved during the recession of the 1980s. Giving employees greater opportunities to participate in decision making also remains an important goal in the 1980s, but while it was considered a quality of work life issue ten years ago, it is now regarded as an essential managerial technique for improving productivity and quality of work output.

Current Challenges

Since we are already well into the 1980s, the new challenges are already with us. The most compelling of these, so far, has been the recession of 1981–82 . Perhaps more important than the recession itself was its duration. Was it unnecessarily prolonged by high interest rates or were there more profound structural changes at work? Another challenge of the eighties is the Reagan administration's philosophy, calling for greater reliance on private enterprise and decentralized solutions of social problems rather than for a continuously expanding federal involvement. What effect will the lifting of federal pressure have on affirmative action efforts in business and other institutions in our society? Another drastic change is the drop in the rate of inflation. Is this drop merely a temporary result of economic distress or has the lid really been put on this Pandora's box? The composition of the labor force is also changing.

The number of young persons entering the labor force will diminish over the next decade or so. The number in the prime productivity age group (25 to 54) will increase sharply during the same period. No one knows for sure what the elderly will do, but if past and present trends continue, the elderly work force will remain constant "as the decline in labor force participation rates offsets the increase in the elderly population."[11] The number of white-collar workers, working mothers, and better-educated employees will also increase. The relative reduction in the number of blue-collar workers will cause a decrease in the membership of large industrial unions.

All of these changes will have an effect on the shape of personnel interests and activities in the decade to come.

Increasing Competition in Business

Of all the changes, however, none is more important than those that are occurring or already have occurred in the competitive environment of business. Since the personnel issues of the 1980s will largely be shaped by management's efforts to compete both domestically and overseas, I should like to focus my attention on the emerging environment of business competition and its effects on managerial strategies and policies. I shall base my observations in part on interviews that I have conducted with Conference Board staff and members of corporate personnel staffs around the country. I shall also draw on my own personal experiences as a director of a smokestack-related business headquartered in New York.

Pessimistic View of American Competitive Strength

In this view, the last recession with its attendant unemployment, particularly in smokestack industries, was more than a cyclical phenomenon prolonged by high interest rates. Pessimistic observers contend that American industry is losing jobs and markets to foreign competition because of a lack of productivity gains in the last decade and the poor quality of its output. Their views are confirmed in the results of myriad special studies reported by the Joint Economic Committee of the Congress of the United States. For example, Jack Grayson, chairman of the American Productivity Center, in a paper included in Volume 10 of the Joint Economic Committee's *Special Study on Economic Change* (1980), describes the problem, as he sees it, in stark terms: "We are in a national economic crisis which threatens not only the future standard of living but also our very survival as a world power."

He goes on to say that "there has been a collapse in productivity growth which began in the mid-1960s and accelerated rapidly after the 1973 oil shock." His figures indicate that the U.S. private business economy had sharp declines in the growth rate of both labor and capital productivity after 1973 and actual productivity decreases in 1978 and the first half of 1979. This dismal performance has resulted, says Grayson, in an "alarming decline in the competitiveness of the United States in the international markets." His figures show that we have lost ground to practically every industrial nation in the world except perhaps Italy and Canada. In 1970, our exports of manufactured goods were about even with those of West Germany. In 1979, West German exports exceeded ours by 29 percent. In 1970, Japan's export of manufactured goods was 62 percent of ours; in 1979, they were 85 percent of ours.

Optimistic View

This pessimistic view of U.S. competitive failure is countered by other more optimistic observers who reassuringly tell us that although the United States is losing its mass production and smokestack industries to foreign competition, it is gaining a whole new set of industries that will take the place of the old. This view is not particularly new and has appeared in a number of guises in the past—for example, the concept of the postindustrial society, a society that has solved its problems of production and freed its people to devote their attention to service-oriented and presumably more creative pursuits.[12] Sociologists also used to discuss the leisure society, and books were written about what things would be like in a society of abundance.

Even earlier, Colin Clark, distinguished economist, developed the thesis that "in the course of economic growth, a country's occupational structure shifts...from primary to secondary to tertiary industries."[13] This, as we know, is exactly where the U.S occupational structure has been heading for many years. Even with the decreasing productivity of the past decade, the number of persons employed in service industries has been increasing sharply, while manufacturing has been barely holding its own.[14] The greatest percentage of growth has been in health, welfare, and religious services. If present trends continue, the largest gains in employment will be among janitors, nurses aids, sales clerks, waiters and waitresses, general clerks, nurses, and food preparation and service workers—not a very exciting future for many of us. The fastest growing job opportunities, however, will be for data processing machine mechanics, paralegal personnel, computer systems analysts, computer operators, office machine and cash register service people, and computer programmers.

Underlying the optimism of those who predicted the

development of a postindustrial society was the belief that automation and greatly increased productivity would reduce the number of employees needed in the factories and free them for other, perhaps nobler, pursuits. A parallel was drawn with agriculture, which once employed more than 90 percent of the work force but, as a result of phenomenal productivity improvements, was able to reduce the percentage required to a current 3 to 4 percent. Unfortunately, if we can believe the figures, no such phenomenal breakthroughs have occurred in manufacturing, at least in recent years, and the diminished number of persons employed in that sector is probably more a result of the exporting of jobs than of their elimination through improved technology.

The older notion of postindustrialism has given way to the vision of an information or knowledge society.[15] We are told that the future belongs to the knowledge industries and to the related activities of knowledge generation and knowledge communication. Presumably, as this theory goes, the United States with its superior science, entrepreneurial spirit, creativity, and head-start in the computer business (not to mention the help the futurists are providing in pointing the way) will recover the dominance it enjoyed in the industrial society of the 1950s. So, if Michigan's auto industry is depressed and more than 10 percent of the citizens of eighteen states are unemployed, don't worry. These workers are merely going through a structural change that will shortly elevate them (if we can only improve the educational system and we *can*, of course, through *automation*) from blue-collar jobs to white-collar positions, from the assembly line to the computer, and from the dirty, old factory to a nice, clean office.

I find myself subscribing partially to both the pessimistic and the optimistic interpretations of our present industrial plight. I don't have any doubts at all that our costs of production exceed those of some other countries and that productivity and cost control are major problems of American management. At the same time, there are in fact new and fast-growing industries with profit margins and growth potential that make the older competitive industries look like the New York subway system. My own view is that American management is quite properly responding to both challenges. It is not, on the one hand, struggling to keep a buggy whip business going by increasing productivity and lowering costs, totally unaware that the market for buggy whips went out with the horses. Nor is it precipitously abandoning existing businesses to embrace the new. In fact, it is very much aware of the dynamics of product/market life cycles in which some businesses are declining while others are in ascendancy, and it sees its major job as managing in an orderly way the phasing out of old businesses and the development of new.

Intensified Competition

Perhaps the most significant fact about the modern competitive scene is not so much the apparent drop in productivity or the apparent success of some overseas industrial countries but rather the speeding up of the product life-cycle process and the increasing efficiency with which companies compete with one another. No longer can new products be introduced and new markets opened up with the prospect of relatively long periods of growth and development. A product/market moves through the developmental phase with alarming speed, attracting competitors like bees to honey, and precipitating competitive turbulence, aggressive marketing, costly product differentiation, add-on services, and price cutting that quickly separates the men (read women) from the boys (read girls).

A good example is the home video game business that started from scratch in 1977 with two competitors and exploded into an estimated $3.8 billion business at retail in 1982 with at least seven major competitors and many lesser rivals seeking various niches. In the first few years, sales in home video games were very modest, but in 1980 they moved into high gear and began attracting the attention of big companies as well as entrepreneurs. By 1982, the situation could easily have been classified as "competitively turbulent," with the older companies expanding their lines to catch wider segments of the market and keep up with the new products being introduced by competitors; with greatly expanded advertising, estimated at $200 million; with patent infringement suits; with price cutting; and with considerably reduced profits.[16]

Of course, the home video game business could be a fad, but even more substantial industries have taken on a faddish quality in recent years. What we think of as fads, after all, are only greatly accelerated product life cycles.

Management's Strategic Concerns

A major consideration in international competition is that there are now many companies out there that can challenge our biggest corporations. This creates considerable turbulence in many U.S. markets that have for many years been stabilized by dominant domestic companies. Of the fifty largest industrial companies in the world, twenty-two are U.S. corporations. Any of these can be challenged by foreign competitors, not only in West Germany and Japan, but in a growing number of other countries as well.[17] The notion that the United States can seize and control new lines of businesses, such as the so-called "knowledge" industry or any other distinct segment of international business without immediate, formidable challenge does not take into account the enormous capabilities of overseas corporations. Even so, competition from overseas is no different in kind from domestic competition.

The management strategy that will dominate both domestic and international competition over the next decade will be one of searching for entry into new and expanding businesses and defending older established ones. The search for new entry will take the familiar form of acquisitions and mergers as well as entrepreneurial adventures. The defense of older, established businesses will be focused on cost reduction, price competition, quality improvements, customer service, and control of markets. These two strategic thrusts will largely determine the shape of personnel concerns during the foreseeable future.

While it is easy to sketch in broad outline the major dimensions of the problems of business competition that personnel and other functional areas will be dealing with in the 1980s, it is considerably more difficult to specify issues that must be addressed in meeting these challenges. From this point on, then, my comments will necessarily be even more speculative.

Trend Toward Sharing Responsibility

The first consideration that comes to mind is that cost and price competition will mean greatly decreased profit margins and a considerable narrowing of the freedom to make mistakes. As a result, management will find that making the wrong decision will be increasingly risky. We can expect, therefore, two responses. The first is a trend toward the sharing of decision-making responsibility. The solitary entrepreneurial genius at the top, single-handedly guiding his enterprise, will be viewed as more foolhardy than heroic. Accordingly, we can expect the increasing involvement of others with a stake in the enterprise, including directors, executives, middle management, and employees. This of course means an enlargement of present planning efforts. Personnel departments will play an important role in designing organizations that obtain the best flow of information and the most opportunities to share the responsibilities of decision making. There may be sharp breaks with traditional hierarchical forms of organizations and a greater reliance on the free flow of information and group processes in decision making. The focus will be on enlisting the widest possible support for company strategic goals and quicker, more flexible responses to competitive challenges.

Trend Toward Intolerance of Avoidable Errors

The narrowing of the freedom to make mistakes will also have the effect of decreasing management's tolerance for "just plain goofs" that could have been avoided. I can remember that a number of years ago we believed that the only way to train a manager was to let him make mistakes. Those were the days when the profit margins were wide enough to tolerate this kind of training on the job. Today, the success and failure of a business cannot be left in the hands of amateurs who are learning as they go. There is too much information available to permit a continuation of the muddling approach of yesteryear. Moreover, intolerance of mistakes could lead to continuing executive turnover. Personnel departments will be called on to provide managerial talent for this grist mill through more effective staffing systems.

The Quest for Lower Direct Labor and Overhead Costs

One area that is likely to receive a good deal of attention in management development programs will be the management of the production function. For a number of years, management development programs have been aimed at expanding the horizons of managers and focusing their attention on financial and marketing goals and the allocation and coordination of company resources to achieve those goals. There will continue to be a need for top executives with broad integrative views but, in addition, there will be an equal need for highly professional, task-oriented managers who are primarily concerned with getting the job done in the least costly and most efficient way.

Production-orientation, however, does not mean a return to Taylorism. The new breed of production manager and efficiency expert will be concerned not only with the work process but with the profit statement and balance sheet as well. One objective will be that of reducing fixed and overhead costs to a minimum so that the costs of production can vary with the business cycle. This will require increasing adaptability and flexibility of machines and men alike. It could mean a greatly reduced number of employees in jobs that cannot vary with the business cycle. Indeed, one prospect is that production knowledge will be built into computers, thereby obviating the need to store knowledge in human beings and making possible the elimination of an entire cadre of expensive knowledge workers.

There are likely also to be great pressures to reduce the costs of direct labor. The cost of labor is not so much in the hourly rate (although that is an important factor in some industries) but in the archaic work practices that are designed to protect jobs rather than to enhance the competitive position of the company. Personnel staffs will be called on more and more to initiate creative new approaches to breaking down occupational rigidities and resistances to job improvements.

These new approaches are likely to involve basic changes in the relation of employees to the organization. Since the concern with work rules and feather-bedding in general originally grew out of fear of job loss, this fear must be removed or accepted as a fact of life before employees will be willing to alter work-rule restrictions in order to increase productivity. One way to eliminate such concerns is through guaranteed lifetime employment. Single-business firms will find it difficult to make guarantees of this kind, but multiple-business firms may be able to do so since they can shift employees from a line of business where sales are diminishing to one where sales are growing. It seems more likely, however, that some way needs to be developed to tie unemployment compensation to the creation of opportunities for displaced employees to move into new lines of endeavor.

The Japanese focus on quality control circles is likely to be emulated widely because quality control is considerably less controversial to employees and their unions than productivity improvement, which has been equated with "speed-up" and the elimination of jobs. No one can argue against high-quality products, yet a reduction in scrap and the necessity for rework directly reduce costs and increase output. Moreover, improvements in product quality may result in unexpected improvements in production methods. Still further, greatly enhanced product quality may give a company the competitive edge it needs to increase sales and command higher prices for its products.

Certain areas of the country may provide greater opportunities for new approaches to the elimination of work-rule rigidities than others. The Southeast, with its more recent industrialization and newer factory organizations, could have advantages over other areas where industrialization has been established longer, factories are older, and work rules are more entrenched. There is a chance in the South for a wholly new approach to management-employee relations built on mutual trust and a desire for consensus rather than for agreements that are hammered out on an anvil of conflict and adversarial relations. Many companies have moved their production to the South because of its work ethic. The South has a great opportunity to build on this cultural advantage and to become an innovator in management and organization rather than an imitator of existing procedures that may already be outmoded.

One interesting development that I picked up in my conversation with former Conference Board colleagues is that while companies are "lean and mean" as a result of the recession, they have not dropped their organizational development activities. In other words, many innovative approaches to management and organization are no longer viewed as experimental frills but are accepted as practical tools for dealing with tough personnel and organizational problems.

From a strictly employment standpoint, the worst scenario that could develop, if domestic costs remain high, is the actual exporting of machines and jobs from the United States or other high labor cost areas to countries where the costs of labor are low. All industrialized countries, including Japan, are engaged in some deliberate job-exporting. In this scenario, a company exports production but retains control of its markets and distribution networks. This strategy could mean a growing marketing orientation for a number of old-line, smokestack industries. Personnel staffs could well be called on to reorient their thinking from a production mode to a marketing mode and could be required to apply personnel planning and resource development methods to the reorientation of an entire division or company. The drastic effect of such a reorientation on an organization need not be spelled out here, but one can readily visualize the extensive surgery, replacement of key personnel, and retraining that would be required.

Loss of Corporate Identity

Up to this point, we have been primarily discussing the effects of accelerated product life cycles and greatly enhanced competition on management's concern with cost and price competition. We should like to turn now to the equally compelling quest for entry into new and developing businesses. The quest for new businesses, like the concern for costs, is not new to American firms but is being greatly accelerated by the more efficient competitive process characterizing modern industry. The personnel departments of larger companies are already thoroughly familiar with the problems of reorganization that attend acquisitions and mergers, since these appear to be the principal methods used by management today to get into new lines of business. We needn't dwell on the problems of managerial redundancy, of adapting to the dominant company's ways of doing things, and other problems of accommodation. But consider the consequences of a greatly speeded-up process of acquisition and divestiture on a company's sense of purpose!

The modern dynamic corporation is in great danger of totally losing its identity unless deliberate efforts are made to reinterpret corporate missions in plausible ways that can be successfully communicated to employees at all levels. The biggest danger is that employees in the divisional boondocks will have none of the sense of purpose and shared values that are so important in guiding decision making where no explicit policies exist. It will be a very important job of the personnel staff to interpret and communicate the basic culture of the company and to provide a sense of continuity in the midst of continuous change.

Staffing and Organizing the Entrepreneurship

The biggest challenge of all to the personnel department of the next decade will be systematic staffing for entrepreneurship. Corporate America has not been particularly creative in spite of its many successes. Most companies survive on one or two really good ideas. With intensified competition, companies can no longer depend on intermittent flashes of creative insight. They need to be organized for more effective entrepreneurship. Creativity requires effective interaction between problem identifiers and problem solvers. A creative organization requires that the problem identifiers and the problem solvers be brought together. This means continuous interaction between people in the field, people on the shop floor, and professional problem solvers. It also requires a highly developed network of relations outside the company. The personnel department can play a crucial role in developing organizational structures to obtain the best internal interaction. It can also develop more effective means of selecting employees with outstanding problem-solving capabilities who could work directly with the top executive team in its strategic planning efforts.

Summary

We have attempted to identify some of the key issues that personnel departments will face in the 1980s. We started our discourse by reviewing the issues of the 1970s and showing how these have carried over into the 1980s. However, issues are modified by emerging problems. We listed a number of these problems but focused on only one, and that was the greatly enhanced competitive environment in which American business is operating and will continue to operate.

Most of the important human resources issues that must be dealt with by personnel departments in the 1980s and beyond will be shaped by management's increasing concern with entry into and development of growing businesses and with the defense of mature businesses. These concerns will result in greater efforts on the part of management to share the responsibility of risky decisions; increasing intolerance of avoidable mistakes; growing emphasis on truly professional managerial skills; increased executive turnover; redoubled efforts to reduce the costs of indirect and direct labor; the export of production functions to lower-cost areas; a shift from manufacturing to marketing; a speeded-up process of acquisition and divestiture; problems of organizational adjustment and integration; and increased interest in organizing and staffing for creative entrepreneurship.

Endnotes

1. Allen R. Janger, *The Personnel Function: Changing Objectives and Organization* (New York: The Conference Board, 1977).

2. Ruth Gilbert Shaeffer, *Nondiscrimination in Employment and Beyond* (New York: The Conference Board, 1980).

3. William B. Wolf, *The Management of Personnel* (San Francisco: Wadsworth, 1961), 111.

4. Janger, *The Personnel Function*, 40.

5. Ibid., 55.

6. Ibid., 58.

7. Peter F. Drucker, *The Practice of Management* (New York: Harper & Brothers, 1954).

8. Jean-Jacques Servan-Schreiber, *The American Challenge* (New York: Atheneum, 1969).

9. Louis F. Davis and Albert B. Cherns, eds., *The Quality of Work Life*, Vols. 1 and 2 (New York: Free Press, 1975).

10. Janger, *The Personnel Function*, 48.

11. Robert L. Clark and John A. Menefee, "Economic Responses to Demographic Fluctuations," in the Joint Economic Committee of the Congress of the United States, *Special Study on Economic Change,* Vol. 10, *Productivity: The Foundation of Growth* (Washington, D.C.: Government Printing Office, 1980), 18.

12. Daniel Bell, *The Coming of Post-Industrial Society, A Venture in Social Forecasting* (New York: Basic Books, 1973).

13. Colin Clark, *The Conditions of Economic Progress* (London: MacMillan, 1957).

14. Thomas Nardone, "The Job Outlook in Brief," *Occupational Outlook Quarterly* (Spring 1982).

15. John Naisbitt, *Megatrends: Ten New Directions Transforming Our Lives* (New York: Warner Books, 1982).

16. Peter Nulty, "Video Games: Why the Craze Won't Quit," *Fortune*, 15 November 1982, 14.

17. "The Largest Industrial Companies in the World," *Fortune*, 23 August 1981, 181.

CHAPTER SIX

Cooperation or Conflict: Southern Labor-Management Relations in the 1980s

BRUCE RAYNOR

Vice President, Amalgamated Clothing
and Textile Workers Union

Introduction

Labor-management relations in this country have a long history of faddish ideas that sweep the literature but seem to wind up having much less effect on real world events. The current state of mind in this field is no exception. We hear much about Japanese management techniques, quality circles, concession bargaining, the decline of the American labor movement, "enlightened" union-free personnel policies, and so forth.

It is worth taking a careful look at these and other developments in order to prepare ourselves for the balance of the 1980s. In past years, the Southeast was far behind the rest of the country in these types of developments. However, we are now moving squarely toward the center of modern thought, even if we haven't quite gotten there yet. Therefore, we must still make an effort to assess the national impact of events and to determine whether that assessment changes when applied to the Southeast.

In addition, the Southeast has some unique characteristics in terms of labor-management relations and the economy in general. It is dominated, though decreasingly so, by the textile, furniture, apparel, and wood-related industries. These are traditionally low-wage areas of employment characterized by locally powerful and paternalistic companies. Also, the South has yet to overcome its problems of racial discrimination and, in particular, the relegation of blacks to the lowest paying industrial work.

If we are to engage in crystal ball gazing, it might be useful to keep in mind that in this field most past predictions have proven to be erroneous. Those scholars who forecast the disappearance of unions in the 1920s were red-faced in the next decade. The prognosticators who prophesied a new era of labor-management cooperation in the 1930s and mid-1940s were shocked by the strike wave of 1946. On this basis, it might be well to warn those modern thinkers who have declared unions to be as outmoded as some of the products of U.S. industry that their conclusions might be premature. Also, those commentators who draw quick and far-reaching conclusions from concession bargaining should beware of potential embarrassment. It is clear that despite enlightened management, workers still need representation in order to get treated fairly. Therefore, unions will play an important role in the southern states in the 1980s.

The solution to the many complex industrial relations questions facing the South obviously lies in labor-management cooperation. Only through mutual give and take will real solutions be achieved. Unfortunately, the basis of trust that is necessary between unions and corporate officials does not now exist in the Southeast and is unlikely to develop in the next few years. Constructive labor-management cooperation will not take place when the rights of unions to exist as institutions are being challenged in the workplace and in the legislative halls. The prospects for the 1980s are for increased confrontation and hostility between the owners of the economy and those who actually produce the wealth.

This discussion will outline the major responses that employers have made in dealing with current problems in industrial relations. The attitude of corporate decision makers toward unions, the way in which they relate to labor organization, and the style of management representation in labor relations will all be analyzed. We will then examine the response of organized labor to current problems in industrial relations. We will focus on labor's initiatives in gaining increased economic power and the internal structural changes wrought by these developments. The major impact of these courses, charted by labor and management respectively, will be seen most vividly in the collective bargaining process. Therefore, we will look at such major bargaining issues as quality circles and Japanese management techniques, technology and productivity, group health insurance, concession bargaining, and trends in government regulation.

Membership Trends in the Southeast

We have heard much about the supposed decline in the union movement in terms of membership, strength, and influence. During the 1970s, membership in unions and employer associations in the United States increased from 21.2 million to 22.4 million (see Exhibit 1). However, the percentage of union membership in nonagricultural establishments declined from 30.9 percent in 1970 to 25.2 percent in 1980. The figures for the Southeast show a marked similarity to national trends. In all but South Carolina, union and employee association membership increased during the 1970s. The total gain in membership in the region was more than 300,000. In percentages, however, the rate of unionization declined in five of the seven states in the region.

How we evaluate absolute numerical increases against percentage declines should be influenced by some major developments taking place in our economy during that period. The severe decline of certain basic industrial sectors that were union strongholds—underground coal mining, tire manufacturing, men's clothing, television manufacturing, and newspaper production—decreased union membership. The severe decline of the industrial base in the Northeast and Midwest at the expense of rapid growth in the Sunbelt, which has not been as well organized, also served to reduce total union membership. A third major factor has been the incredible rise in management hostility to unions, resulting in a

---

Exhibit 1: **Trends in Unionization in the Southeast**

Union and Association Membership (in thousands)	*1970*	*1980*
United States	21,248	22,366
Alabama	228	296
Georgia	273	323
North Carolina	167	228
South Carolina	98	93
Tennessee	312	334
Florida	348	420
Mississippi	86	135
Percent Unionized*		
United States	30.9%	25.2%
Georgia	22.6	21.8
North Carolina	17.5	15.1
South Carolina	11.6	7.8
Tennessee	23.5	19.3
Florida	16.2	11.8
Mississippi	14.9	16.2

---

*Union and association membership as a percent of nonagricultural employment

Source: Bureau of National Affairs, *Directory of U.S. Labor Organizations*, 1982–83 ed.; Bureau of Labor Statistics, *Directory of National Unions and Employee Associations, 1971* (Washington, D.C.: Government Printing Office).

---

major shift in company attitudes toward the organization of new plants. The "southern" strategy of many large corporations that had previously been neutral on the issue of union contracts at new facilities became one of intense opposition. The widely publicized increase in attempts to dislodge existing unions through professional decertification campaigns also hurt union membership. Another crucial element in this equation was the rise of multi-industry conglomerates, which became much less vulnerable to pressure from individual unions and therefore were free to expand the nonunion portion of the business at the expense of union plants. One example is General Electric's southern expansion.

All of these factors and others should account for a drastic decline in the strength of unions. However, the facts show a numerical increase nationally and in the Southeast. A percentage decline may reflect shifts toward public employment and service-oriented industries and the decline of basic manufacturing and construction as the dominant influences in our economy. We are therefore left with the feeling that it is amazing that the labor movement survived the 1970s intact.

Obviously the losses in manufacturing and construction membership were offset by the gains in union organization among white-collar and government workers. Union membership in the public sector grew from 5.8 percent of the work force in 1958 to 16.7 percent in 1978. It is important to note that with the exception of Florida, government workers on the state and local levels remain largely unorganized in the South. The labor movement has replaced tire builders and automobile workers with teachers and secretaries. This is a trend we can expect to continue through the 1980s as the industrial structure of the American economy continues to evolve.

As AFL-CIO President Lane Kirkland said at the 1981 AFL-CIO Convention, "The makeup of this body bears little resemblance to the Horse Collar Workers, the Architectural Cornice Makers, the Box Sawyers and the Nailers and the Umbrella and Walking Stick Makers who gathered into the federation a hundred years ago. This body will bear as little resemblance to those who assemble under our banner a hundred years hence."[1] The labor movement has always reflected the economy and there is little evidence to suggest that this will change.

The Response of Management

It is misleading to generalize about this complex American institution. There are as many divergent attitudes, opinions, and styles of conduct among the decision makers of our private industries as there are in the society we live in. The backward personnel policies of Texas Instruments and the progressive stance of Xerox are good examples of the range of opinions. Winn Dixie's neanderthal attitude toward unions stands in startling contrast to most of the other major supermarket chains. We can only identify some major trends, but keep in mind that there are many exceptions to every generalization.

Milton Derber, the president of the Industrial Relations Research Association and a professor at the Institute of Labor and Industrial Relations at the University of Illinois, noted that, "Most U.S. employers and managers have accepted unions and collective bargaining out of necessity, rather than conviction, and have perceived union participation in decision making as a burdensome infringement on their functions and rights."[2] The only proviso I would add to Derber's remark is that only a minority of corporate decision makers *have* accepted collective bargaining as a part of our democratic system. American management has never been convinced that unions are a necessary and important part of a free democratic society. In recent years many leaders of corporate America have initiated a new offensive to see if unions can be severely weakened or even destroyed.

The one characteristic I find most common in U.S. employers is a short-run view of the world. Our companies operate to produce a dividend every quarter and a steady growth of profits. Long-term planning and programming seem remarkably absent from corporate practice. Periodic layoffs of workers are more common in this country than anywhere in the world. I have heard many company executives complain of excessive costs involved in bumping, which is a direct result of the ups and downs of employment levels in an industrial plant. American industry has kept its relationship to the educational system at arms-length. Industry leaders support political candidates who are least likely to significantly upgrade the school systems. Then these same corporate leaders complain that there will be a shortage of workers to operate the advanced machinery entering our factories at an increasing rate. This contradiction is due to a world view and day-to-day conduct based almost solely on next quarter's results. A candidate who raises taxes to improve the schools will hurt next quarter's profit, although it will lead to higher profits in the next decade. Unfortunately, taking the long-run viewpoint is not the way the system works.

This short-term view of the world has yielded a set of attitudes with which we can readily identify. American management fundamentally doesn't accept unions unless there is *no other choice*. Southern management is even more radical about unionism. Some major southern corporations would prefer to permanently injure their company than deal with a labor union. The classic example of this philosophy is the historic seventeen-year battle between the Amalgamated Clothing and Textile Workers Union and the J. P. Stevens Company. The company spent millions of dollars more to fight the union than it would have cost the company to settle. Management severely weakened the company rather than accept collective bargaining. Another classic example has been the efforts of the United Steel Workers and the AFL-CIO Industrial Union Department to organize Florida Steel. Despite millions of dollars spent by this employer and possible irreparable harm to the company, the war continues after more than a decade of conflict.

There is no reason to expect that this subtle hostility to bitter opposition of southern management will change in the 1980s. More companies in the Southeast are and will be controlled by national and multinational corporations in the coming years, however. This should slightly shift the orientation of southern management toward the national center during the balance of this decade. Fewer Roger Millikens and more Chicago- and New York-based chief executive officers will determine the approach of southern management in the 1980s. However, deep-seated opposition to unions will certainly continue throughout the Southeast.

Management Consultants—Attorneys

A large industry of management consultants, in many cases lawyers, has evolved, specializing in matters relating to unions, equal opportunity, and general personnel decisions. Nationally, but particularly in the South, these individuals and firms have become increasingly influential in determining management's decisions in these areas. With the unfortunate increase in the legalization of labor relations, these law firms have grown enormously in the last decade. In the Southeast, most of these firms are Atlanta-based and keep growing and splitting like some microscopic creature. This development will surely continue to have a profound effect on industrial relations in the 1980s.

The self-interest of these people is union-management conflict, litigation, and fear on the part of managers about impending union organization. For example, it would be financially foolish for a lawyer to advise his client that since a union has won a National Labor Relations Board (NLRB) election, it would be proper to negotiate a mutually acceptable collective bargaining agreement. By opposing the election results through litigation, a law firm is able to bill its clients large amounts of money. If they still lose, the next step is to convince a client that unionization would be a disaster to the entire company, that the union has no staying power, that it will lead to organizing campaigns at other plants, and so forth. This effort at persuasion, if successful, will result in long, involved negotiations in an attempt not to reach an agreement. Again, large fees at the bargaining table result because the client is convinced his executives can't handle this job alone and need the presence of an outside labor lawyer. Also, large fees are collected through the lengthy NLRB and court procedures. This scenario can go on until either the employer wins and the union withdraws or someone in the company finally wakes up and sees that he or she is busy fighting unions instead of making money and worrying about the economic future of the company.

It is also in the self-interest of lawyers and consulting firms to keep managers and executives afraid of the impending union menace. Hence, the development of elaborate seminars to advertise their services for problems they have convinced companies that they have. This field of law creates its own demand and expands to fill it in the best traditions of our free enterprise system. The only problem is, however, that the self-interest of a particular company may well be different from that of the lawyers. Numerous companies have been permanently injured by a failure to understand why their lawyers advised them to fight the union for as long and in the way that they did.

The myth gets perpetuated one step further when, after a company finally makes up its mind to live with a union, the lawyers convince their clients that they are a necessary ingredient in the relationship. Of course, for a substantial retainer the outside lawyer can maximize arbitrations, create periodic crises, and encourage management to distrust the union. All of this creates a continued source of income for the law firm.

If the influence of this industry on southern management

continues to grow, we can predict increased conflict, litigation, and confrontation because that is what these lawyers need in order to stay in business. I have seen these lawyers incapable of resolving conflicts even when management wishes to, simply because, like Pavlov's dogs, they salivate at the presence of a union. However, it is possible that the self-interest of the corporations will override the southern management lawyer's drive for legal fees. This would entail more in-house representation by companies and the entrance of more national management law firms who earn their livelihood by representing clients who bargain with unions and pride themselves on reducing conflict. To my knowledge, there is not a single large management law firm in the Southeast who would fall into this category. In my experience, several southern law firms do not have a single lawyer who even knows how to establish a bargaining relationship with a union.

Cooperation—Only When There Is No Other Choice

Another basic tenet of American management is that co-operation with unions is great but "only if you have to." In the 1960s and 1970s, General Motors (GM) developed its southern strategy and set up nonunion plants in Georgia, Alabama, and Louisiana. They provided these workers with the same basic wage and benefit structure as their union workers but spent additional energy and money developing internal practices to stay union free. Some plants were organized when the United Automobile Workers forced the company to sign a neutrality pledge at the bargaining table. Finally, in concession bargaining GM agreed to recognize the union without elections at the last four nonunion southern plants This decision was based strictly on the union's insistence that in order for GM to get what it wanted in bargaining, it would have to abandon its southern strategy. Similar examples can be found in the negotiations relating to nonunion southern plants between some of the major tire manufacturers and the United Rubber Workers.

Many union leaders are excessively suspicious of management, and it is commonly believed by union leaders that "they only want to work with us when they want something or when they have no other choice." Another aspect of this problem is the schizophrenia of management. When the textile manufacturers in the South want to fight in Congress for import restrictions, they have no difficulty standing shoulder-to-shoulder with organized labor. However, that cooperation to save jobs and their companies doesn't extend outside the foreign trade negotiating rooms. If real cooperation is ever to be achieved, management must work with labor more consistently on a voluntary basis.

Labor's Response

American labor leaders see trouble on the horizon. Our traditional bases are rapidly being eroded in the steel, automobile, rubber, construction, and other industries. The labor movement is naturally experiencing profound change and this should continue through the 1980s in several major areas.

Unions and Politics

Labor has survived the doomsayers on the left and the right. It has withstood the assaults of antilabor administrations and Congresses before and will certainly survive the present one. However, survival does not mean continuation of the status quo. The AFL-CIO has drifted leftward politically in recent years and should move more so in that direction. Equally as important as external events was the end of the reign of George Meany. Meany ran the AFL-CIO Executive Council and tolerated little dissension from his own strongly held opinions. To mold a politically diverse group of fiercely independent International Union presidents into a viable policymaking body for the labor movement was a herculean task. Meany did that with his national stature and strength of will.

Despite the strengths of Lane Kirkland, the present AFL-CIO president has a much different historical role to play. Having waited so long to exercise its independence, the AFL-CIO Executive Council is coming to the fore as the decision-making body of the American labor movement. There is now a strong leftward move among several major International Union presidents. Joining International Association of Machinists (IAM) President William Wimpisinger in advocating a more radical approach to corporate America are powerful presidents of the American Federation of

State, County, and Municipal Employees (AFSCME), United Automobile Workers (UAW), United Food and Commercial Workers Union (UFCWU), Amalgamated Clothing and Textile Workers Union (ACTWU), and the Communications Workers of America (CWA). This assertive executive council will increasingly become a vehicle for more creative and radical approaches by the labor movement. On occasion we shouldn't be surprised to find the president of the United Mineworkers of America (UMWA), Rich Trumpka, adding his union's weight to various offensives. Without Meany's strong hands on the helm, the AFL-CIO will drift leftward throughout the 1980s.

Two examples of this development were the AFL-CIO's positions, and those of many unions, on the nuclear freeze issue and defense spending. Long-held support for defense spending, the cold war, and nuclear weapons programs are being reappraised. Many union leaders will never return to the position that any new weapon the Pentagon wants automatically has union support. Even such unions as the UAW and the IAM, whose members directly depend on Defense Department orders, have altered their approach by discussing the need for "socially productive" investments.

In addition to vicious corporate attacks on organized labor at the plant level during recent years, the right-wing assault in the political arena has become a second front. With longtime union hater Orrin Hatch as chairman of the U.S. Senate Labor Committee and the rise of other right-wing types in the Congress and the executive branch, the attack has begun in a new arena. While we were used to attacks on the minimum wage every few years that included a youth subminimum provision and the like, no one was prepared to see the Occupational Safety and Health Administration (OSHA) dismantled, openly antiunion appointments to the NLRB, and proposals to destroy longtime safeguards, such as the Davis Bacon prevailing wage law. However, many labor leaders who were not convinced that we were under attack at the job site, store, and factory, have become angered as a result of the current legislative and administrative assault on the labor movement.

This galvanizing of the labor leadership and the radicalization of the entire movement is a growing reality. We are supporting legislation to limit corporations' rights to close plants, to provide government jobs, to reindustrialize our basic industries, to protect our domestic industries through tariffs, and many others. I would expect a much more far-reaching effort to reform the National Labor Relations Act (NRLA) than our last attempt in the late 1970s. More and more unions have now had bitter personal experiences with employers willing to throw caution to the wind during organizing campaigns. The list of corporate symbols of recalcitrant management is now quite long and spans a wide range of American industries and fields of employment.

While this more radical type of legislative program obviously won't succeed in the present Congress, the labor movement is actively working with other groups to elect a more pro-labor national legislature. Union leaders have now taken a leading role in the national Democratic Party as well as in the state and local levels. This more partisan role will substantially increase labor's ability to influence politicians in coming years.

Labor and the Economy

In order to make any progress unions have been forced to overcome intense employer hostility to union organizing at the plant level and weak federal labor laws. That dilemma has led to some new approaches that are as usable in times of peace as they are in conflict. Through the much-publicized corporate campaigns that ACTWU used against J. P. Stevens and several other companies, the entire area of union financial clout has been opened up. Pension funds have become the largest single source of capital in this country and are now worth over $600 billion.[3] They hold approximately 25 percent of the stock equity in U.S. corporations and 40 percent of the corporate bonds.[4] Much of the influence over, if not direct control of, these funds is in the hands of the labor movement. With their backs to the wall in the area of organizing and the steady erosion of their northeastern and midwestern bases, the unions will increasingly make use of this potentially explosive weapon against corporate America. In concert with other sympathetic institutional investors, such as churches and universities, the potential to pressure corporation management is enormous.

Although there are currently some major legal blocks against this sort of labor offensive, these are only a bill away from reality. As a report issued by the corporate planning division of the American

Telephone and Telegraph Company states, "The concept of property rights in pension fund contributions has several important implications. If workers have such rights, then, by extension, they are owners of pension fund assets.... This would then mean that pension participants, through their funds, would own what could amount to a controlling interest in most large American corporations."[5]

While there is no immediate danger that plumbers, bakers, and steelworkers will be sitting in the corporate suites in the 1980s, there should be at least two distinct areas of expansion of union activity. The first is already underway. Union-influenced or -controlled funds have provided financing for unionized industries to expand. The Marine Engineers Beneficial Association (MEBA) pension fund has put up $11 million to partially finance the construction of two new ships that will sail with union crews.[6] Building trades unions have in numerous instances provided financing to put their members to work. In its first two months of operation, a union consortium in southern California provided over $30 million in capital for four union-built construction projects. A similar effort in the Chicago area has produced $13 million, with a total of $50 to $100 million expected to be available for union contractors.[7] While southern unions don't directly control many large local and area pension funds, this type of funding to provide union jobs could become significant in the future years in the South.

Obviously, a major area of potential clout lies with the large public employee pension funds. These will be especially useful because of the expanding aggressive unions in the public sector such as the American Federation of Teachers (AFT), Service Employers International Union (SEIU), CWA, and AFSCME, whose members have a bargaining relationship with these funds. According to a study done by the AFL-CIO Public Employee Department, more than $150 billion is controlled by the fifty largest public employee pension funds, and more than $250 billion is carried in all the public employee funds.[8] Of the groups contained in the fifty largest funds, the overwhelming majority of the covered workers are represented by unions.

While the effort to create union jobs has begun, there is another major direction that is much more tentative. This is the use of pension funds, along with allies, to pressure major corporations. It has now become almost commonplace for labor unions to have representatives and their allies at stockholders' meetings to challenge management on antiunion actions. While presently we are wielding relatively small numbers of shares, the problem of size is solvable in the next few years. Labor is already advancing proposals to liberalize the ERISA to allow limited use of these funds. One proposal developed by the AFL-CIO Industrial Union Department Committee on Pension and Benefits Policy identifies some sound investments as:

1. Residential mortgages and other investments that promote the development of communities in which fund beneficiaries work and live.

2. Firms with large domestic work forces.

3. Firms that have good labor relations records and support their employees' organizational rights under national labor laws.

This proposal involves the creation of a federal agency similar to the Federal Housing Authority (FHA) that would guarantee certain investments made from pension funds.[9] Many other proposals are floating around, and we can look for general support to develop around one in the next few years. By whatever means, the pressure labor can put on corporations outside the confines of the factory, job site, or store is potentially more powerful than any weapon labor has ever possessed because it strikes at the heart of the power of America's corporations.

The South can be particularly important in this effort because this is the location of many of the battlegrounds for present, past, and future organizational efforts. Management law firms in the South will be placed in a difficult position because their best advertisement has been their success at withstanding unions at the plant gates. When it is time for corporate leaders to settle in response to outside pressures and plant level efforts, these lawyers will be like fish out of water and will be frequently omitted as part of the settlement.

Labor's Internal Changes

Shedding many of its old images and prejudices, the labor movement is becoming more professional. More and more labor leaders are educated and well read. Union organizers were once hired only from the shop floor after working their way up from stewards. Today we find more and more unions hiring dedicated young people out of the universities. As the nature of the unionized work force is changing, this will affect the people representing organized labor. As the work force becomes better educated so do the staffs. As steelworkers make up a smaller percentage of union members and as membership of white-collar workers increases, the character of the union representatives also will change. Unions such as CWA, SEIU, National Union of Healthcare Employees, and the UFCWU have been in the forefront of these changes.

This upgrading of union representatives will show itself in more aggressive and creative organizing approaches. It will result in more planning and pressuring of the employers away from the plant gate. It will result in a strengthened alliance with labor's natural allies in the intellectual community, among civil rights groups, and in the churches.

Another basic change that has been under way for several years is the union merger movement. Many present-day unions are the product of mergers of smaller organizations. The ACTWU is composed of four previously separate unions, and the UFCWA is another good example of a labor conglomerate. As unions merge, they become more capable of sustaining battles with corporations. Mergers inject new vigor into organizations that have lost their drive; they inject new life into the American labor movement. These mergers also streamline the operations of unions and allow them to run more efficiently. In addition, and probably equally as important, mergers concentrate the real power in the hands of fewer organizations and therefore will make labor better able to act in concert.

Collective Bargaining in the 1980s

Quality Circles and Japanese Management Techniques

The most prominent development in labor-management relations in recent years has been the advent of quality circles in all their various forms. We can expect this fad to continue through the remainder of the decade. Many companies and some unions have adopted a set of ideas related to humanizing the work environment and providing channels for worker input into the production process. In many instances these developments have produced more talk and scholarly papers than real action in the workplaces of America, but, nevertheless, this concept will be of increasing importance in the next few years.

One of the basic tenets of the quality circle approach to increasing worker involvement is a cooperative, nonadversarial relationship between the union and the company. In the Southeast this approach will continue to run into serious difficulty. Many unionized southern employers still harbor a desire to either weaken or defeat the union that represents their workers. In many cases, the same employers who wish to develop a quality circle program at a unionized facility also have nonunion operations where they take an aggressive antiunion position. On this contradiction these programs will usually falter. Even after quality circle programs begin, if the union and the employer get into a battle at another location, the obvious reaction of union leaders will be to either directly or indirectly destroy the cooperative programs in the unionized locations.

Another pitfall for the quality circle movement will be the character of American corporate management. Because of the drive for quick results in the profit figures for the next quarter and, at most, the next year, the long-term commitment required by such a program won't be there in most cases. When U.S. Secretary of Labor William Usury asked Japanese managers whether quality circles would work in the United States, they told him no, because "American managers don't have the necessary patience."[10] A good example of this phenomenon has been the reaction of many corporations to embryonic quality circle programs when the recent economic recession deepened. Many put the programs on hold or simply turned them into programs to improve the quality of the product and scrapped all the "junk" about worker involvement. The bottom-line mentality of American management ultimately categorizes the worker-involvement side of quality circles as a luxury one can do without.

As a Toyota executive stated in a speech about the differences between the American and Japanese automobile industries, "At

Toyota, we have fifteen fundamental management guidelines that we take very seriously. The first fourteen of those guidelines deal in one way or another with human relations and how to treat our people; the fifteenth is profit maximization. At the U.S. auto companies, profit maximization is Number One."[11] There are few American companies that do not fit this apt description.

An additional major problem for American management in successfully selling this concept to the labor movement and convincing union leaders that there is no hidden agenda has been the widespread use of the quality circle as a device to keep workplaces union free. This is not a use the programs have been put to in Japan but is a "creative" response that is peculiarly American. A good example of this use was the effort by General Motors in their aborted "Southern Strategy." They implemented quality of work life (QWL) programs in nonunion plants in Georgia, Alabama, and Mississippi. Many UAW leaders felt this was clearly an effort to frustrate union organizing drives. As a result, despite the UAW's highly publicized support of QWL programs at General Motors, there are mixed feelings, at best, within that union about them.[12] Because the UAW has been the staunchest union supporter of the QWL concept, its continued leadership will be crucial if labor is to maintain at least an open mind on the subject.

Another good example of the use of quality circle programs to frustrate union organizing drives is the approach developed by Johnson & Johnson (J&J). This company has a very sophisticated QWL program designed to keep the ACTWU out of its southeastern and southwestern plants. At a new J&J facility in Albuquerque, New Mexico, the company has developed quality circle teams with spokespeople chosen for each group. Through the spokespeople, the group is expected to evaluate fellow workers along many different lines. For example, circle members are expected to report to their leader about the mistakes fellow group members make. One of the criteria for evaluation in the J&J system is company loyalty, which of course is translatable into antiunion sentiment. However, the developers of this use of quality circles did not anticipate the rebellion of workers against this type of manipulation by management. That rebellion has produced substantial union support among many J&J workers.[13]

Other imported Japanese management techniques will continue

to receive attention from American corporations as the result of the tremendous success of Japanese companies. Without examining each technique, we can categorize them as ways to increase the level of cooperation with the work force and make workers feel a part of the success or failure of a company. This type of management encourages workers to take pride in their company and its products, leading to increased quality and productivity.

However, there are many tangible differences between our industries and system of industrial relations and those in Japan. These differences make the quality circle approach largely unworkable in the United States. One important factor is that Japanese factories were built after World War II and are therefore much more modern than ours. For instance, we hear of the large wage differential between American and Japanese steelworkers. However, we do not hear as much about the widespread use of basic oxygen furnaces in Japan as opposed to the open hearth furnaces in this country. The same comparison can readily be made of the use of shuttleless looms in Japan as opposed to the still-dominant but outmoded shuttle loom in the U.S. textile industry. Another major difference is the two classes of workers common in Japan: full-time and part-time. Nippon Steel employs only 42 percent as many workers as does U.S. Steel, but those figures belie the thousands of less fortunate workers who are either employed part-time or for subcontractors. Industry in the United States, on the other hand, has a history of employing a full-time work force and using subcontractors only as a special approach to certain types of maintenance and construction work.[14]

In labor relations we find as many differences as there are similarities. Japanese unions are organized vertically by company as opposed to our labor organizations, which operate on an industry-wide basis. While the Japanese unions are not what we would call company unions, there is a blurring of the lines between union and management. Many management representatives were once union leaders or may still be union members. That cultural link may be as responsible for a cooperative relationship as any formal programs we read about. In the Southeast even more than in the rest of the country, there is a sharp cultural difference between management and workers. The system of private clubs for executives and other professionals provides a very clear class difference between workers and management all through the South. The cultural, racial, and class distinctions between management and workers in the South certainly are major factors in increasing the degree of hostility between unions and companies.

A good example of the difficulty of importing Japanese management techniques to this country and the Southeast in particular has been the record of union opposition by Japanese companies that have built plants here. The much-publicized desire of Nissan to operate their Smyrna, Tennessee, automobile plant as nonunion has done more to make American unions suspicious of Japanese management techniques than all the QWL consultants combined.

By and large, Japanese companies have attempted to operate nonunion in the Southeast and have fallen easily into the pattern of their American counterparts. They retain the same Atlanta law firms and use the same vicious tactics to oppose the efforts of their workers to organize. One example was the successful attempt of YKK Zipper in Macon, Georgia, to decertify the Cement, Lime, and Gypsum workers after a first contract.

In the experience of the textile industry, we have found that Japanese company executives frequently want to rid the plant of imported practices once a plant is organized. During contract negotiations with a Japanese company in Macon, Georgia, the company attempted to eliminate sick days, seniority bonuses, and merit raises and to install our familiar attendance discipline systems and equal pay for equal work concepts. An interesting side note to this particular situation was the spectacle of a Japanese manager delivering a tough captive-audience speech before the NLRB election while wearing his *zen zen dome* (Japanese textile worker's union jacket). If he didn't find a contradiction in that action, the ACTWU organizers certainly did.

While we will see the growth of the Japanese phenomenon in U.S. labor relations, we will also see its ultimate failure. As hostilities in the Southeast continue, unions will be less and less disposed to trust the motives and intentions of management. Even in Japan, the quality circle movement involves only a small minority of workers and is considered coercive by many unions.[15] For the

Southeast, our conclusion is that since U.S. corporations have never accepted the legitimate role of unions, these cooperative techniques will ultimately be unsuccessful.

Technology and Productivity

It is vital to our industrial base that major advances in technology and capital equipment take place throughout this decade in order to compete with countries offering lower wages and boasting modern plants and equipment. Our corporations will not survive in the international marketplace without such effort and must obviously depend on the commitment of corporations to spend the millions of dollars necessary to modernize our industries. While this is a positive, necessary, and likely development, it will create many problems for industrial relations directors and union negotiators.

Generally, most union leaders now appreciate the importance of new technology and more efficient work practices. However, the attitude of local union officials, shop stewards, and rank-and-file members is more suspicious. They have the natural resistance to change that is common throughout all levels of society. Any company official who becomes frustrated over union members' resistance to changing workloads and job content when new equipment is introduced ought to see the trauma of supervisors learning to operate under a collective bargaining agreement for the first time. This resistance can and will be overcome, however, if a cooperative relationship is developed with the union.

In terms of employment in the Southeast, the textile industry is still dominant and will be so for at least the remainder of the 1980s and probably beyond. Modernization has already begun in earnest in this main industry of the South and has yielded positive results. According to David Tracy, vice chairman of J. P. Stevens, "The American textile industry has spent a great deal to modernize and now it is Number One. We produce twice the amount of goods per man hour as any other country does, and this will improve." He also noted that "the U.S. is way ahead of Number Two, South Korea."[16] In fact, the American textile industry leads all other domestic manufacturing categories in productivity growth rates.[17]

However, continued growth in productivity involves more than simply capital investment and must include an equally substantial human investment as well. Companies will have to pay special attention to the effects that changes in equipment have on the jobs of employees. This should entail a positive effort to improve relations with employees and the unions that represent them if there is to be any success. In a national poll conducted for the LTV Corporation by Opinion Research Corporation of Princeton, New Jersey, "500 U.S. opinion leaders" expected and favored a more cooperative relationship between unions and employers.[18] This will certainly prove to be a necessary prerequisite for the continued improvement in productivity sought by southern management in the 1980s. What sense will it make to spend multimillions of dollars on new equipment and lose a substantial percentage of that benefit through labor-management hostilities?

The most convenient scapegoats for low U.S. productivity are lazy, unionized, well-paid factory workers. As labor relations directors will see in the next few years, there is another culprit as well. From 1977 to 1980 American production rose 7.9 percent, adjusted for inflation, while blue-collar employment gained only 2 percent. At the same time, white-collar employment rose 12 percent. Less than 600,000 new blue-collar workers entered our work force, but 5.5 million professional and technical white-collar workers entered our corporations.[19]

In negotiations, union leaders will expect to know what the company has done about the ranks of the supervising group and the front office when management seeks productivity changes. It is the common perception among union members and many union leaders that while management wants more work, advanced skills, and cooperation from workers in order to trim costs, any discussion of extra management baggage is another story. The number of supervisory personnel, for example is considered by companies to be a topic that is legally and, more importantly, conceptually off-limits when it comes time to discuss ways to increase the competitiveness of the plants. However, the legal separation doesn't hold up when workers see the ranks of the white-collar workers grow while they are asked to cooperatively adapt to new equipment and techniques. Equality of change will be an important component of industrial relations in the 1980s.

Negotiating Health Insurance

Health care costs have been rising rapidly over the past few years and are going to become an increasing problem for unions and companies in the years ahead. In 1977 the average insurance premium for southern workers amounted to approximately $500 per year, of which 72.2 percent was paid by employers. While this was about $100 per year less than the national average, a more startling statistic was that southern employers were paying anywhere from 10 percent to 15 percent less in comparison to companies in other regions.[20] In other words, southern workers were getting poorer coverage and paying more for it than workers in other parts of the country.

As health care costs rise by large percentages in coming years, we can expect severe bargaining crises for union and company negotiators. Further, we can expect a major effort by southern unions to bring their health care packages, in terms of coverage and employee costs, up to national standards. This issue has already become a major problem in negotiations in the southern textile industry.

Obviously, the solution to this problem once again lies in a cooperative relationship between unions and employers. The recent appearance in other parts of the country of health maintenance organizations specializing in preventive health care will go a long way toward reducing the burdensome cost of health insurance. Another effort that is desperately needed in the Southeast are multi-union and multi-employer coalitions to provide better care and lower costs. Melvin Glasser, former UAW director of social services, contends that local coalitions are an "interim" solution to control health care costs. These coalitions can provide the influence necessary to force the medical profession to cooperate in improving preventive health care and to find creative solutions to decreasing the length of hospital stays and providing more office procedures.[21] This problem is a common one for labor and management and is only going to be solved by a cooperative effort. While the labor movement will continue its long-term efforts to install a system of national health insurance, we can do much in the short run to solve this serious problem.

Concession Bargaining

Much has been said and written about the advent of concession bargaining in the last few years. This development, brought on by the severe economic crisis in our society, is having its biggest impact on basic unionized industries—automobile, trucking, construction, rubber, and steel. While this change has been very significant for union-management relations, one must be careful in predicting a continued wave of union acquiescence to freezes and givebacks demanded by management at the bargaining table. For example, Chrysler workers refused to agree to another contract without provisions to regain some of their lost money from a previous concession contract. In fact, in many industries the concession movement never got started. In textiles, despite pay increases that have been lower than in previous years, there was no general backward movement or even freezes in wages. According to the Bureau of Labor Statistics, excluding the automobile and trucking industries, the average 1982 wage gain for all industries was 7.8 percent.[22]

We can predict, however, that management will continue for some time to attempt to negotiate concession contracts. This will likely lead to strikes and other forms of conflict as union members who may have yielded once will feel that they are owed a return for their past sacrifices.

Potential benefits can accrue to corporations and unions alike if we can use some of the creative approaches developed out of the necessities of concession bargaining. Such concepts as gain sharing that emerged in the last few years have potential for building a common interest between union workers and companies. While this is immediately attractive to management, it must include expanded benefits if labor is to cooperate. Most experts emphasize that for gain sharing to work it must include increased job security, job training, and worker participation.[23] To really identify with management goals, workers must feel that they have input into decision making and some tangible measure of whatever success is achieved. Further work can be done on tying extra wage increases to productivity if the plan is designed to give workers some control over its success or failure.

The real danger of our recent wave of concessionary contracts is the reaction of workers when the overall economy or even the performance of a particular company improves. Workers will remember the position they were forced into by company negotiatiors, and we can expect them to react accordingly. One of the most serious mistakes some companies have made was to demand concessions even though they were not economically necessary. This "riding the tide" by companies who take advantage of the defensive position of organized labor is a very dangerous game to play. If one takes a longer-term view we know that the swing of the pendulum will once more put unions in a powerful position in their collective bargaining relationships with employers, and the day of reversing the roles may not be far away. At that time we can expect to hear company executives and their friends in the southern political structure complaining about unreasonable wages and benefits being forced on them by powerful unions.

Government Regulations

Regulations imposed by the federal government on southern employers in the areas of occupational health and racial and sexual equality should continue to occupy an important place in labor-management relations. Despite the current administration's efforts, we can expect little fundamental change in the national policy of using government force to guarantee a safe workplace and equality on the job. Since the Reagan administration took office— amid vows to dismantle burdensome regulations that had been accumulating since the New Deal—little basic change has taken place. The only telling blows that have been struck are in the areas of administering the safety and equality laws. At best these are short-term reprieves for companies and will have little lasting effect.

Negotiators in the balance of the 1980s will still have to carefully construct ways to provide a safe and healthy workplace. This issue has been one that pits unions and companies as adversaries. Perhaps as the problem is accepted by industry as one that won't disappear, both sides of the bargaining table will learn to constructively reduce the health risks workers face on the job. Unions will become more concerned with health problems in the 1980s, and negotiators will grapple with such issues as chemical information, engineering controls on substances, and transfers of workers designated as having medical problems. These issues can be resolved at the bargaining table, and perhaps we will see less litigation and more cooperative action in this whole area.

Equality at the workplace is still a major problem for industry in this country and the Southeast in particular. Black workers will continue to press companies for equal treatment and, most importantly, equality in the better-paying jobs. Since blacks still overwhelmingly support unions in the South, they make up a disproportionate number of union members and activists. This will continue to pose problems for southern management in undoing the results of past discrimination. Most major employers in the textile industry have already paid off at least one major EEOC lawsuit but still have not fundamentally altered their system of excluding black workers from many promotional opportunities. Because of the attitudes of most lower-level southern managers, we cannot foresee any basic change in the coming years. Unfortunately, this issue most likely will continue to be fought out in the courts with new, record-setting settlements appearing each year. Unions may wind up in the forefront of promoting these lawsuits against union and nonunion employers both as a means of self-defense and as an offensive weapon. The increasingly close alliance between labor and the civil rights movement may well result in more common legal efforts to force employers to correct past discrimination.

Conclusion: A Decade of Conflict

Every major free industrial nation has a strong labor movement, and the United States is certainly no exception. That will be borne out in the years ahead. However, hope springs eternal in the hearts of corporate America that organizations of workers will somehow become outmoded. We are presently in a period when national management thinkers and their advisers are once again saying that labor is on the decline permanently as a force in this country. That is not only a false sense of security but is also a dangerous way to conduct business for the next few years. The strength and size of our labor movement has historically been cyclical. While labor is undoubtedly in a defensive position, the signs of a change are already appearing. One good barometer is the end of the much-heralded rise of decertification elections in recent years.

The intensity of attacks on unions has been an enlightening and radicalizing experience for the labor movement. Unions that long thought they had good relationships with major industries have seen these companies expand their nonunion southern plants while allowing their unionized facilities to become noncompetitive due to a lack of capital investment. Companies with union and nonunion facilities can expect some hard bargaining in the 1980s over neutrality clauses and recognition of the union at other plants. Another major area of conflict will be the conduct of company campaigns against unions. Unions will no longer allow the confines of the battle to be plant sites and NLRB proceedings but will seek more creative means of pressuring employers on a national level. This will be particularly difficult for southern management, which has traditionally been allowed to break all rules in keeping labor unions out of their local plants.

Unless there is a marked change in the legislative agenda of the various industry associations and the U.S. Chamber of Commerce, we can expect more ambitious legislative and political pushes by the labor movement. Although unsuccessful up to this time, efforts have been made to dismantle legislation that labor has viewed as sacred cornerstones of our society. This will provoke a reaction that will see labor playing a more active role in politics and making some far-reaching proposals to amend the nation's labor laws.

Because of the influx of foreign-owned plants into the Southeast, labor has been forced to pay more attention to international ties to other unions. Labor movements in the United States and Japan are developing a closeness that will certainly affect the actions of Japanese employers in the Southeast in their labor relations policies. The traditional ties to the European unions will result in more international efforts to pressure multinational corporations in bargaining and organizing. The UAW-Nissan battle in Smyrna, Tennessee, may well be won or lost far beyond the state boundaries.

The fundamental factor in southern labor relations will

ultimately be the role played by the influential management law firms. The success of these groups depends on conflict between unions and employers. It is much more lucrative for a law firm to convince a client that a principle right of the employer is being challenged and that costly litigation is necessary than for the parties to resolve issues at the bargaining table. To further their own interests, therefore, lawyers seek to convince management that company officials are incapable of properly handling their own labor matters. If this group continues to play a dominant role in southern labor relations, we can predict an intensification of the conflict. When the region's basic industries such as textile, furniture, wood, and construction fully recover from the most recent recession, workers in nonunion plants and work sites will be demanding union organization. The results of this new round of organizing and its effects on the already unionized companies will largely depend on the character of the employer opposition. That in turn is going to depend on the role that chief executives of major corporations allow the southern management law firms to play.

Therefore one can say that the events of the 1980s will be determined by the players and the roles they are allowed to play. The response and direction the labor movement is being forced to take is clear. Let's hope that it doesn't lead to destructive conflict for our economy, our region, and our society. Let's hope that business decisions in the corporate boardrooms will overcome ideology and fear and that a new era of creative solutions to common problems in the workplace and the economy will dawn for unions and companies. The opportunities are there for constructive cooperation in the Southeast if we all choose to take advantage of them.

Endnotes

1. Lane Kirkland, "Preparing Ourselves to Serve the Future," *The AFL-CIO American Federationist* (December 1981): 1.

2. "Debates on Changes in Collective Bargaining," *Labor Relations Reporter* (10 January 1981): 3.

3. "AT&T Studies Union Interest in Pension Investments," *Labor & Investments* 1 (April 1981): 3.

4. Jeremy Rifkin and Randy Barber, *The North Will Rise Again* (Boston: Beacon Press, 1978), 10.

5. "AT&T Studies Union Interest," 3.

6. "MEBA Fund to Finance Two Ships," *Labor & Investments* 1 (January 1981): 3.

7. "Funds Target Investment in Union-Built Houses," *Labor & Investments* 2 (June 1982): 1.

8. "Public Employee Department Conducting Pension Study," *Labor & Investments* 2 (May 1982): 4.

9. "ACTWU Officers Proposes National Pension Program," *Labor & Investments* 2 (November 1982): 1, 6.

10. "Criticism Voiced of U.S. Managements Approach..." *BNA Daily Labor Report*, no. 95, C-1, 17 May 1982.

11. Ibid., C-2, C-3.

12. "Labor: Hot UAW Issue: Quality of Work Life," *Business Week*, 17 September 1979, 120-121.

13. James N. Ellenberger, "Japanese Management: Myth or Magic," *AFL-CIO American Federationist* (April-June 1982): 4.

14. Ibid.

15. Ibid.

16. S. Gray Maycumber, "Mill Execs Pin Hope on Productivity," *Daily News Records*, 16 April 1982.

17. Machinery & Allied Products Institute, *Capital Goods Review* (April 1982).

18. "LTV Poll of Labor, Management Leaders," *Labor Relations Reporter* (13 September 1982): 111LRR33.

19. Lester C. Thurow, "Why Productivity Falls," *Newsweek*, 24 August 1981, 63.

20. U.S. Department of Health & Human Services, *Health: United States*, DHHS Pub. no. (PHS) 82-1232 (Hyattsville, Maryland, December 1981), 87-88.

21. "Health Care Costs and Business Labor Coalitions," *Labor Relations Reporter* (13 September 1982): 111LRR37.

22. Beth Brophy, "More!" *Forbes*, 7 June 1982, 42.

23. John Hoerr, "Why Labor and Management Are Both Buying Profit-Sharing," *Business Week*, 10 January 1983, 84.

CHAPTER SEVEN

Labor Relations Issues Facing the Southeast in the 1980s

CURTIS MACK

The Law Firm of Mack, Caldwell, Steckel, and Nelson
Atlanta, Georgia

Introduction

I have been asked to address the critical labor relations issues facing the Southeast in the 1980s. The issues I have chosen, for the most part, are not limited to the South—they affect all regions of the country and have impact on businesses and unions almost across the board. The topics are:

1. The movement of businesses to the South and the potential problems of union-management adversarial positions.

2. Major organizing drives by the AFL-CIO in the South.

3. "Corrective" bargaining.

4. Instability at the NLRB.

5. Controversy surrounding management's use of the polygraph examination.

Moving South

Southern Growth

Throughout the 1970s, economic, political, and social factors led to a population and employment boom in the South, generally at the expense of the Northeast and North Central regions.[1] Such regional movement has been attributed to many sources, including the South's comparatively low tax rates, low levels of public assistance, and somewhat restrictive labor legislation.

A 1975 study that monitored business starts, growth, and relocations rated states on the favorability of their business environments. Seven of the twelve "best" states were from the South: Texas, Alabama, Virginia, South Carolina, North Carolina, Florida, and Mississippi. Seven of the "worst" were from the Northeast: New York, Massachusetts, Delaware, Connecticut, Pennsylvania, Vermont, and New Jersey.[2]

Among other factors that may have influenced, and may continue to influence, moves to the South are the relatively union-free climate of Sunbelt states, the existence of right-to-work laws in nearly every Sunbelt state, and the growing worker population. The states of the Northeast have also been hurt by relatively high labor costs there. Further, major cities in the North have been victims of chronic decay and a general decline in the quality of life. Taxes in northern states, both corporate and individual, remain among the highest in the nation. Northeastern states, particularly New York and New Jersey, have also been hotbeds of unionism for years, and legislatures have provided more and more laws that benefit workers at the expense of management. Thus, the North, which is in an advanced stage of industrial development, has begun to sag under the weight of government regulation, population overcrowding, and worker demands.

The Role of Unions

In contrast to what may be called a type of rugged individualism among southern workers, the North's unionized work force has become almost an outside party in labor-management relations.

Workers seek safety through the union contract. The labor-management experience in the North has generally evolved to the point where unions and management have assumed arms-length, almost antagonistic attitudes toward each other. It is often only a pending major catastrophe that can spur meaningful dialogue between the parties.

One illustrative example of such discussions occurred with the *New York Daily News*. After the paper was on the verge of collapse, agreements between its unions and its publishers—aimed at reducing labor costs by $50 million each year—were reached and resulted in the paper's continuation. Another northern newspaper was not so lucky. *The Philadelphia Journal* stopped publication in 1982 after losing $15 million dollars in four years. It closed its doors after the company's requests for wage and staffing concessions were rejected. Apparently, the needed medicine was too much for the workers to swallow. Instead, about 125 employees lost their jobs.

The Lesson for the South

The South is enjoying a sustained period of business growth. New industries locate here, old industries expand, and many industries from other regions look to the South as a refuge. So far, things look quite good. They look good for Southern business and look tempting for unions as well. But we should learn some lessons from the experiences of the Northeast. Businesses are moving South for reasons. The appeal of the South is a product of interconnected geographical, economic, political, and legislative characteristics that set it apart from other regions. We must be careful not to emulate other areas that at one time enjoyed the advantages we have now.

Particularly, it is important to maintain a climate that continues to attract business to our area. Thus, low taxes, reasonable employment laws, and relative freedom from union control should remain characteristics of our region. Even for those advocating the expansion of unions, it is important for management and labor to avoid the depersonalized, arms-length relationship that has developed in the North.

As more bargaining relationships emerge, care must also be taken to avoid adversarial relationships. Further, management and labor should not conduct business based on short-term indicators of prosperity or growth. Unions should avoid looking for the "quick-kill" in favorable economic terms, while management should be flexible enough to realize that coexistence is far better than extinction. Such lessons were learned too late in many regions. We should ensure that the same thing does not happen in the South.

The Southern Targets

The AFL-CIO Effort

With its membership base continuing to erode, organized labor has begun an all-out effort to revive itself by mounting intensive, heavily financed organizing drives throughout the country in virtually every sector of business. Frustrated by its failure to increase power through political channels as it settles into the 1980s, the labor movement is reverting more and more to its original method of fortifying itself by organizing workers.

Not surprisingly, labor's organizational strategies have grown more sophisticated. As an example, consider the AFL-CIO's decision to increase monthly dues and use a large portion of that money to establish a "labor institute for public affairs." Concentrating on commercial, cable, and satellite television, the AFL-CIO institute tries to bolster the image of unions through advertising and public affairs programs. The AFL-CIO has apparently budgeted approximately $5 million for this advertising campaign.

New Organizing Campaigns

In October 1981, the AFL-CIO launched a major project to organize workers in Houston, Texas, and throughout the Sunbelt. Union officials have consistently noted that Houston presented an ideal location for organizing. Many new firms, for example, have located in Houston, while the city already harbors numerous older businesses that the unions contend pay lower wages, provide few benefits, and offer limited job security. Further, Texas ranks about forty-eighth nationally in the percentage of unionized workers, and the AFL-CIO claims a potential for about 800,000 new union members in the Houston area alone. Among the prime targets of the organizing drive are health care institutions, the public sector, and the construction industry.

How successful was the campaign? It depends on who you listen to. From January 1982 through April 1982 the AFL-CIO claimed to have added between 2,000 and 2,500 employees to its membership roll. The numbers included about 1,000 construction workers and 1,200 public employees. By December 1982 unions claimed between 5,000 and 6,000 new members.

In the context of a massive representation effort for 800,000 workers, it is at least arguable that things did not go exactly according to the AFL CIO plans. While AFL-CIO President Lane Kirkland was quoted as being "quite satisfied" with the campaign, others have acknowledged that their gains "are not enormous" and are "by no means a great figure."[3]

What slowed the movement in Houston? Among other things, Texas is a right-to-work state that prohibits contracts requiring union membership as a condition of continued employment. Thus, in the contracts they negotiate unions are precluded from insisting on a variety of union security clauses that are commonplace in states without right-to-work laws. Further, companies took postures with the help of attorneys and consultants well-versed in the art of resisting organizational efforts. Also, in the early 1980s Houston had begun to feel the impact of the recession, with the unemployment rate rising from 4 to 8 percent in about one year.

Interestingly, the concerted activities of members of one union slowed the fight for representation in another union. The Hotel Employees and Service Employees' Unions targeted the Astrodome sports complex for a concerted organizing drive. The unions sought to represent cleaning workers, ushers, security guards, and parking lot attendants at the Astrodome. However, the drive was stalled by a National Football League Players strike that left the stadium empty of fans, players, and employees alike.

What does the future hold for Houston? The Hotel and Service Employees' Unions renewed the battle once the baseball season began. Kirkland acknowledged, "We're here for the long pull."[4] The AFL-CIO has invested significant sums of money and sought much publicity for its campaign. Thus, expect a slow death for union organizing in Houston—if for no other reason than as a face-saving measure.

A second AFL-CIO organizing campaign is being conducted in the Atlanta area. According to leaders of the AFL-CIO's Industrial Union Department, Atlanta's relatively union-free environment and its status as a big-time industrial city make it fertile ground for organizing efforts. Efforts to organize workers in Atlanta have combined the forces of the Amalgamated Clothing and Textile Workers, United Food and Commercial Workers, Carpenters and Joiners, International Ladies Garment Workers Union, American Federation of Government Employees, and the Service Employees' Union to focus on industrial, service, and white-collar workers.

Since early 1982, when Atlanta's unionized work force numbered approximately 70,000, unions have had only limited success in their organizing drives. As in Houston, the AFL-CIO has seen some gains in the public sector arena but has met stiff resistance in private industry.

A third city targeted by organized labor is Washington, D.C. In June 1982 the Coalition of Labor Union Women, in conjunction with the AFL-CIO, launched a drive to organize women employed in nongovernment clerical, technical, and professional jobs in and around the nation's capital. The campaign initially was directed at approximately fifty nonunion employers, including health care institutions, retail stores, high tech industries, and factories. The campaign was aimed specifically at the estimated 300,000 nonunionized women with jobs in private industries.

"Corrective" Bargaining

The National Labor Relations Act (NLRA) was passed in 1935 in the depths of the depression. One of its main purposes was to provide equality of bargaining power to employees. The method of achieving this objective was to encourage collective bargaining. Some forty-seven years later, in the midst of a recession, attention again turned to equalizing bargaining power. But of course in 1982 there was a big difference. It had become necessary to give some aid and comfort to management. The method again used was collective bargaining or, perhaps more precisely, "corrective" bargaining.

The most publicized concessions have resulted from negotiations between the United Auto Workers and the car manufacturers. These included a freeze in wages, suspension of the cost-of-living escalator, and elimination of twenty-six paid holidays.

Despite the auto concessions, immediate adjustment of contract terms was not the only consequence of attempted corrective bargaining. In 1982, Chrysler workers overwhelmingly rejected a contract settlement that had been agreed to by the company and the UAW leadership—marking the first time the rank-and-file split with the union leadership and rejected a proposed contract at one of the major automakers. More than 70 percent of the company's hourly workers voted against the proposed contract, which called for cost-of-living raises that would have added an estimated 5 percent or 50 cents an hour to the average worker's pay by June 1983. The workers wanted an immediate raise. Chrysler refused to grant the immediate pay hike, almost daring its workers to strike. Under these circumstances, the Chrysler workers voted to stay on the job and postpone negotiations on a new contract until January 1983. That approach had been pushed by UAW President Douglas Fraser, who reasoned that an improved U.S. economy and increased auto sales in the fall of 1982 might put Chrysler in a more generous mood in 1983. Chrysler's 10,000 Canadian workers were less patient and went on strike, resulting in the layoff of thousands of American workers.

Concessions have also been won in other industries. The big meat packers—Armour, Swift, Wilson, and Oscar Mayer, for example—obtained an agreement that included a freeze on wages at least until September 1984 COLA (cost-of-living adjustment) payments were deferred until December 1983. Likewise, some supermarket chains were able to gain reduced labor costs. One of the most drastic and dramatic concessions was achieved by A&P in Philadelphia. The company agreed to keep some stores open that it had planned to close in exchange for a $2 per hour reduction in pay. The most remarkable aspect of this agreement was that it provided for the eventual purchase of the stores by the employees. (The company agreed to set aside 1 percent of gross sales for this purpose.)

There are tens and even hundreds of other examples of companies that have successfully obtained relief from the unions with which they deal. However, these numbers give a distorted picture of what is happening in this country. For every situation in which a company has been successful, there is probably one, or five, or even ten, where the company has not obtained "takebacks." One of the most disquieting examples of this was the rejection by the United Steelworkers Union of any concessions in 1982. The industry had requested an early opening of the agreement which was due to expire in 1983. This midterm request for relief was overwhelmingly rejected by the Steelworkers' membership. Steel's depression worsened, with mills operating at about 40 percent of capacity and nearly half the industry's hourly work force on layoff.

Intransigence by union members is not limited to the Steelworkers. Some employees in the supermarket industry have rejected any reductions in pay or benefits, despite a plea that stores and warehouses would close. In a number of cases such as Baltimore (ACME Supermarkets) and Altoona (A&P), facilities were closed. At Iowa Beef, a strike over concessions ended after four and one-half months. Workers returned to work at the same wages they were paid before the strike.

Communications

A company's ability to succeed in corrective bargaining will probably require payment of a corresponding price. The price may be providing employees with greater job security. The price will certainly be the expenditure of time to communicate with employees. Employees will accept reductions only if they understand the need for them. Educating employees with respect to a company's financial status is a first step. It is no wonder General Motors employees in 1982 agreed to concessions by only a razor-thin margin. They were under the mistaken impression that the company made money that year. In fact, the company lost $560 million dollars. Worse yet, when the company tried to explain this, the employees disbelieved it. So, ongoing communications are essential in setting the stage for corrective bargaining. And those communications must be credible.

However, a recent case illustrates that all the communication in the world will not overcome an intransigent union and a National Labor Relations Board (NLRB) that limits management flexibility. In *Milwaukee Springs*, 265 NLRB No. 28 (1982), a company sought midterm wage concessions from the union that represented its workers. The company cited a $200,000 per month decline in revenue as the basis for its difficulty and explained to the union that it would have to relocate its operation to a nonunionized facility if some concessions were not made. After discussing its difficulties with the union and calculating a compromise wage proposal, the company and the union discussed the circumstances that would trigger the company's decision to relocate and the effects it would have on employees. The company claimed that money was the issue and that relocation or wage concessions would solve the problem. The union and company failed to agree on a compromise solution, and the company proceeded to transfer its operation and lay off more than thirty workers.

The NLRB found that the company's action violated sections 8(a)(1), (3) and (5) of the NLRA and ordered the company, *inter alia*, to reopen its old facility, take back its workers, and provide back pay to those who had been laid off. Thus, a company in financial difficulty sought relief, exercised sound business judgment, and was then, in essence, ordered to continue to suffer financially.

While we may be seeing the beginning of the end of this period of concession bargaining, I believe there will always be opportunities for companies to engage in corrective bargaining, depending on their particular circumstances. Despite cases like *Milwaukee Springs*, a realistic, nonantagonistic approach to bargaining and the corresponding communication that results may be the most significant elements of all.

Politics and the Board—The Breeding of Instability

The NLRB has been getting it from all sides. Management attorneys, union attorneys, and a former board chairman have decried the elaborate and often frustrating process of appointing members to the NLRB. Members of the Federal Bar Association expressed concern that "the continuing game of musical chairs at [the] NLRB has produced instability and uncertainty that makes it difficult to assess what the law is at any given moment."[5]

The "musical chairs" to which the association referred stems from the appointment procedures for members of the NLRB. The NLRB provides a staggered system of appointments, usually for terms of five years, which is intended to avoid an administrative housecleaning by a newly elected president. Theoretically, at least, such staggered terms ensure continuity of membership on the board and hence, consistent decisions, even if administrations change. Because of retirements, resignations, and rejected appointments, however, practice has not conformed to theory.

A quick look at recent changes at the board provides insight into how the system operates. By the end of 1982, President Reagan had three opportunities to alter the ideological makeup of the NLRB. He proposed a new chairman of the NLRB and made two membership appointments. Pending Senate approval of his nomination, the president has nominated another attorney to a recess appointment as temporary chairman of the NLRB. Thus, provided his choices win approval by Congress, President Reagan has fashioned a board reasonably in tune with his own labor philosophy.

Should Reagan succeed in changing the ideological composition of the board, what are the consequences? The U.S. Chamber of Commerce hopes for a change from the board's "demonstrated... anti-business bent."[6] Former board general counsel John S. Irving hopes for a change from "the misguided and unbalanced views of members Jenkins and Fanning."[7]

What does such turnover do for confidence in board pronouncements? Very little. What weight should practitioners, business leaders, and unions give to board decisions issued while its membership is in a state of flux? What are the odds that a decision issued in March will be completely reversed in September? Consider just one example of the kind of flip-flop on substantive issues attributable to shifting board membership. In 1962 the board considered the case of *Hollywood Ceramics Co.*[8] That case concerned representation election propaganda and created a board standard for evaluating misleading campaign information against which statements by unions and management would be judged. Essentially, the board evaluated campaign communications and determined whether or not it disrupted the conditions under which a board election should be held. Fifteen years later the board overruled *Hollywood Ceramics* in *Shopping Kart Food Market, Inc.*[9] One year later, *Shopping Kart* was overruled by *General Knit* of California,[10] which reinstituted the *Hollywood Ceramics* rule. Then, in 1982, the board overruled *General Knit* in *Midland National Life Insurance Co.*[11] In essence, these philosophical fluctuations by the board leave unions and employers wondering which way to turn.

Although the *Hollywood Ceramics* history may be extreme, the problem it highlights is certainly common. The political nature of the board brings many forces to bear on its members: political allegiance, intellectual integrity, and personal conscience among them. It is not clear what force has the most influence, nor which should provide the guiding light. It is clear, however, that until American business and union leaders are shown some stability and consistency by the board, its decisions will not provide the guidance necessary to create and maintain industrial peace.

Polygraph Examinations

There is a growing controversy concerning the use of lie detectors to screen job applicants and investigate thefts at the workplace. The polygraph device measures and records involuntary body responses to stress, such as changes in blood pressure, pulse, respiration, and electrical conductivity of the skin. By mechanical/electronic measurement of the subject's physiological reactions to key questions, and comparison of the subject's response to "control" questions, the polygraph examiner interprets those responses in order to detect when a person is lying.

Very often, the polygraph is used by employers to aid in detecting the truthfulness of an employee's job application. As an investigative tool, it can serve to verify or refute a prospective employee's claims. Further, and perhaps essentially, the polygraph is used by employers to prevent or detect theft or other forms of dishonesty by employees. American companies lose billions of dollars each year due to employee dishonesty. In many cases, in order to conduct internal investigations of theft, companies employ the services of polygraph examiners. "Suspects" or others who may provide information on a particular problem or series of problems are questioned about the various incidents. Based on employee responses during the examination, employers attempt to uncover additional leads or discover the culprits involved.

While polygraph examinations may serve a necessary function for employers, use of the exam is not universally condoned. A major argument against the use of the polygraph is the question of reliability. Polygraphers claim the tests are 90 to 95 percent accurate under normal circumstances. However, critics of the test argue that, without years of training and well-developed skills, polygraphers are not equipped to administer and interpret the test properly. Some opponents point to the lack of objective control when an employer subjects an employee to a lie detector test. Still another concern is the lack of licensing or other methods that would assure expertise and safeguard administration and interpretation of the tests. Nor, it is argued, is there assurance that the tests are truly voluntary, since economic considerations may be so strong that an employee has no realistic choice when requested by the employer to take a polygraph exam. Finally, there are constitutionally based arguments, including invasion of privacy and—in the criminal context—the right to remain free from involuntary self-incrimination.

In response to controversy concerning use of the lie detector, many states have increased legislative controls on its use. Currently, an employer who demands or requires that employees or prospective employees submit to a polygraph examination violates the law in eighteen jurisdictions.[12] Penalties for breaking the law range from fines to prison sentences. In some states, such as Connecticut, the mere *request* to submit to a test may be unlawful. In others, like Nebraska, an employee may *consent* to an examination and discontinue the examination at any time. Other jurisdictions (approximately fifteen) neither ban the use of lie detectors nor require polygraphers to be licensed.

Various states that do not impose an outright ban on the use of the polygraph may apply other restrictions. Virginia, Nevada, and New Mexico have laws relating to the use of polygraph examinations but do not completely prohibit such testing. In Virginia, employers are barred from requiring a job applicant to answer questions in a polygraph test about his or her sexual activity, unless the activity has resulted in the applicant's criminal conviction. The Nevada statute prohibits the release of results of a polygraph examination without the consent of the examinee. The New Mexico statute prohibits a polygraph examiner from asking questions related to a person's union affiliation or activity as well as race, sexual affairs, creed, or religion, without the individual's prior written consent.

Particularly in criminal trials, judges have almost universally barred admission of results of lie detector examinations. The chief concern to the judiciary is the lack of consistent, scientific evidence of accuracy. Until such accuracy can be proven, or until the polygraph acquires general acceptance in the scientific community, it is doubtful that the polygraph will be a welcome addition in courts of law.

In the face of growing statutory restriction and with the apparent sympathy of the judiciary, numerous civil suits are being undertaken by employees who claim that they have been improperly discharged from jobs based on polygraph examination results. Among the grounds used for such suits are civil rights laws and tort theories, including product liability, malpractice, defamation, and intentional infliction of emotional distress.

An employer's institution of a requirement that employees take a lie detector test is a mandatory subject of bargaining and, hence, must be discussed with a union representing those employees.[13] Thus, unions have a keen interest in addressing and challenging an employer's polygraph requirements and taking affirmative steps to limit the use of lie detectors. Unions regularly arbitrate cases involving the discharge of employees. When the discharge involves lie detector evidence, unions have met with some success. Some arbitrators have been reluctant to uphold discipline based on polygraph results. Given the inadmissibility of polygraph results as evidence in criminal and civil cases, arbitrators have sometimes applied the same rule to arbitration proceedings. Others have accepted the polygraph as merely one piece of evidence or as supplemental evidence. Even in states where compulsory polygraphing is permitted, arbitrators have not always upheld discipline of an employee who refused to submit to such a test.

Like arbitrators, the NLRB has been hesitant to rely on the results of polygraph examinations in determining whether an employee has engaged in misconduct. Recently, in a case where a test had been unlawfully administered to an employee, an employer was not permitted to rely on evidence arising from that test as a justification for the employee's dismissal, even though it linked the employee to thefts of the company's product.[14]

Something needs to be done to balance the rights of employers to protect themselves from pilferage and the rights of employees to be protected from unjustified action. While the lie detector has not been shown to be 100 percent reliable, its use as an investigative tool is beneficial, nonetheless. Legislatures and unions, particularly, seem unwilling to acknowledge the difficulties of an employer faced with extensive dishonesty among employees. The antagonistic attitude toward employer investigations can cause more harm than good as businesses continue to suffer losses and pass such losses to consumers throughout the country.

Endnotes

1. U.S. Dept. of Labor, *Monthly Labor Review*, "Moving to the Sun: Regional Job Growth, 1968–1978," (March 1980).

2. Ibid., 13.

3. Bureau of National Affairs, *Daily Labor Report*, 10 May 1982, 90, A-9; Union organizing director Alan Kistler and public relations director Dave Paladino, respectively. BNA, *Daily Labor Report* 15 December 1982, 241, A-1.

4. Bureau of National Affairs, *Daily Labor Report*, 10 May 1982, 90, A-9.

5. Bureau of National Affairs, *Daily Labor Report*, 10 September 1982, 176, A-6.

6. Comments of Robert Thompson, Chairman of the U.S. Chamber of Commerce Labor Relations Committee. BNA, *Daily Labor Report*, 17 December 1982, 243, A-1.

7. From *The Survival of the Misguided Majority*, a paper presented by John S. Irving before the Southwest Legal Foundation, reprinted in BNA, *Daily Labor Report*, 26 December 1982, 207, D-1.

8. 140 NLRB 221 (1962).

9. 228 NLRB 1311 (1977).

10. 239 NLRB 619 (1978).

11. 263 NLRB 24 (1982).

12. These jurisdictions are Alaska, California, Connecticut, Delaware, District of Columbia, Hawaii, Idaho, Maryland, Massachusetts, Michigan, Minnesota, Montana, New Jersey, Oregon, Pennsylvania, Rhode Island, and Washington.

13. *Medicenter, Mid-South Hospital,* 221 *Labor Relations Reference Manual* 670 F(NLRB 1975).

14. *Fixtures Manufacturing Corp.*, 251 NLRB 778 (1980).

CHAPTER EIGHT

Conclusion

BRUCE E. KAUFMAN
Professor, Department of Economics,
Georgia State University
WILLIAM T. RUTHERFORD
Professor, Department of Management,
Georgia State University

The assignment we gave our seven authors was to look ahead into the 1980s and identify what they saw as the critical employment issues facing the states of the Southeast. It is evident from reading these papers that they have covered a wide range of topics with a great deal of insight and expertise.

In order that these papers be useful to the widest possible audience, we deliberately included topics that covered all dimensions of the employment relationship. Our authors were also selected so as to bring a variety of viewpoints and backgrounds to the subject. Given the diverse topics and perspectives, it seemed useful to attempt to pull together the major threads from each paper and present a synopsis of what we believe our authors have identified as the critical employment issues of the 1980s. In our opinion, these issues can be grouped into four categories—employment, economic inequality, obstacles to growth, and labor/management relationships.

Employment

The prospects of slower employment growth in the southeast region during the 1980s was perhaps the single largest area of concern among our authors. As detailed in the first three papers by Marshall, Ratajczak, and Robinson, the economy of the southeast region experienced much faster rates of employment growth during the 1970s than did the nation as a whole. Between 1970 and 1980, for example, civilian nonfarm employment grew by 42.8 percent in the states of the Southeast but by only 27.9 percent in the nation.

For a variety of reasons our authors predicted that the pace of job creation in the Southeast during the eighties would slacken significantly, though it would remain above the national average. Ratajczak, for example, foresaw an annual growth in employment in the Southeast during the decade of only 2.5 percent, compared to the 3.7 percent annual increase experienced during the 1970s.

Our authors identified several reasons for this slowdown in employment growth. One view was that the exuberant growth of the 1970s was a "one-time" event associated with the process of convergence between the structure of the regional economy and the national economy. The economies of the southeastern states have historically had a greater concentration of employment in agriculture and nondurable manufacturing and a smaller proportion of jobs in durable manufacturing, finance, services, and trade than has the rest of the nation. A result of this has been that wage rates and per capita income in the Southeast have been significantly below national averages. Robinson, for example, shows that in 1950 per capita income in the state of Georgia was only 70.6 percent of the national average and by 1970 had risen to only 85.2 percent.

Economic theory predicts that labor and capital will flow to the geographic areas where they can earn their highest return. In the view of our authors, therefore, the above-average employment growth experienced by the Southeast was a natural outcome of the inflow of capital into the Southeast during the 1970s, attracted by cheaper labor costs. This flow of capital was also abetted by the reversal in the 1970s of the historic outflow of labor from the South to the North, as population shifts to the Sunbelt created new markets for manufacturing, trade, and services.

While wage rates in the Southeast remain 17 percent below the national average, the process of convergence, in the view of our authors, may lose some of its steam in the 1980s. One reason is the flow of capital to Third World countries. As discussed by Marshall, manufacturers that located in the Southeast to take advantage of lower labor costs are now being attracted by yet lower costs in Mexico and various Asian countries. A second reason is the emergence of high-tech industry as a major source of employment growth in the 1980s. Our authors expressed a common concern that the states of the Southeast might not be able to compete for high technology jobs because of the lower educational and skill levels of the region's work force. Finally, a third source of concern is that the major source of growth in employment in the years ahead is likely to be in nonmanufacturing sectors, such as services and trade, that are tied far more closely to population density. Thus business firms are less likely to migrate to the Southeast because of the allure of lower labor costs.

Besides the slowdown in the process of convergence, our authors also identified several other reasons for potentially slower growth rates in employment. One is that the national economy itself is likely to post only moderate growth rates in the 1980s. This slackening of growth is tied partly to the slower growth rate of the labor force in the eighties as well as to the demand-restraint policies adopted by the Federal Reserve to combat inflation. Ratajczak also points out that the large defense buildup under the Reagan administration will benefit other regions of the country more than the Southeast.

Finally, we are concerned about the threat to regional employment from foreign competition, particularly in the textile and apparel industries. These two industries alone account for over 900,000 jobs in the Southeast. Lower-priced foreign products benefit American consumers but obviously pose a large threat to domestic producers and their employees. Textile and apparel employment will most likely continue to drop, as marginal, high-cost firms are forced out of business by imports. Other industries may indirectly benefit from foreign competition, however, because companies will be forced to increase management efficiency and improve the technology of production through substantial capital investment in new plants and equipment. The net result seen by our authors, however, is a continual slide in employment in these key industries.

Inequality in Economic Outcomes

A second major theme that runs through these seven papers is a concern with the distribution of economic rewards among geographic areas and demographic groups in the Southeast in the 1980s. In particular, our authors are questioning whether the growth in employment and incomes projected to take place in the region will be equally shared.

One aspect of this concern with inequality is the discussion in Ratajczak's paper about the disparate growth prospects facing the states in the South Atlantic area of the region versus those in the East South Central. He argues that during the 1970s the states of Alabama, Mississippi, Kentucky, and Tennessee in the East South Central area did not have the economic convergence that the South Atlantic states of Georgia, the Carolinas, and Florida experienced. In his view, the 1980s will continue to see unbalanced growth as employment opportunities in the East South Central area stagnate, while growth in the trade, service, and finance sectors in the South Atlantic area provide new jobs in those states.

A second area of concern for our authors was the inequality of economic rewards between whites and blacks in the region's population. Maclachlan examined a number of dimensions of economic success for blacks and whites. She found that with respect to labor force participation and employment, black and white men and women in the Southeast were nearly identical to their counterparts in the nation. When she examined various measures of underemployment, however, she found that three out of four of these measures were more severe for blacks in the Southeast. The three measures were involuntary part-time employment, the incidence of workers in poverty households, and the percentage of workers having marginal, low-skill jobs.

Maclachlan also examined the relative positions of blacks and whites in the Southeast with respect to earnings and the incidence of poverty. She found that in 1982 the median usual weekly earnings of black workers in the South were the lowest of all regions in the United States. Black men and women did, however, improve their income position relative to whites slightly during the 1970s. In 1973, the ratio of income of black men to white men in the South was .68, by 1982 it had risen to .70; the income ratio for black women rose from .83 in 1973 to .86 in 1982. With respect to the incidence of poverty, Maclachlan found that the poverty rate for blacks in the South fell from 43 percent in 1970 to 35 percent in 1980. Despite this progress, the poverty rate for blacks in the South was greater than in other regions although, on the positive side, these rates narrowed somewhat during the 1970s.

In assessing the economic prospects for blacks and other low-income workers in the 1980s, however, Marshall is pessimistic that they will be able to continue to improve their position. He relates this to the shift in federal government taxation and expenditure programs under the Reagan administration, the threat to low-wage workers of displacement by foreign competition, and the crowding of illegal immigrants in low-wage labor markets. Marshall also believes that low-wage workers in the Southeast will see their economic position deteriorate relative to other workers because union organization is lower in the region.

Obstacles to Growth

A third issue our authors focused on was the obstacles to more rapid growth in the Southeast region. Probably the issue that received the most attention in this regard was the need for increased management efficiency and labor productivity.

A major theme of several papers was the need for change in the traditional style of management practiced by firms in the Southeast and throughout the nation. Marshall argued, for example, that if firms in the Southeast are to remain competitive with foreign producers they must learn how to use their labor resources more effectively. In particular, he argues that the traditional authoritarian style of management results in lower labor productivity than is achieved with the participatory management systems in Japan and, to a lesser degree, Europe.

Moore expands on this theme in a number of respects in his paper. One challenge to management in the 1980s that he discusses in detail is the growing legal obligation of business firms to provide equal opportunity of employment for women and minority groups. He notes that the increasing intrusion of government into the employment policies of businesses has necessitated a centralization of decision making in personnel departments. According to Moore, a critical issue for management in the 1980s is to devise personnel policies that meet the legal requirements of the equal opportunity law and yet respond to the growing pressures on business for cost competitiveness.

A second area of challenge for management, according to Moore, is the reduction in direct labor and overhead costs. He focuses particularly on the need for removing archaic work practices that restrict productivity. While management may recognize the necessity of such measures, Moore argues that the critical problem is for the personnel department to devise incentives for the employees to cooperate in this effort rather than resist them because they are concerned about their job security. This again echoes Marshall's discussion of the need for a more participative style of management in which workers are treated as more than a factor of production.

A third obstacle to growth in the Southeast focused on in several papers is the inadequacy of the region's educational and training institutions. As Ratajczak and Robinson point out, a large part of the growth in employment in the 1980s will be in white-collar occupations requiring advanced educational attainment; jobs in lower-skill, blue-collar occupations, on the other hand, are expected to have little growth. These authors question whether the southeastern states are investing enough resources into their educational systems to prepare young people to effectively compete for these jobs. Robinson also notes that the lack of a well-educated, skilled labor force is a major deterrent to attracting new high-tech firms into the Southeast.

Conflict or Cooperation in Labor Relations

A fourth critical employment issue identified by our authors concerns the resolution of conflict in the labor-management relationship. A theme sounded by Marshall, Moore, and Raynor is the close link between productivity in the business firm and the style and climate of labor relations. Firms in the Southeast in the 1980s are likely to come under increasingly competitive pressures from other foreign and domestic producers, requiring close attention to cost and productivity.

In our authors' view, a major challenge facing firms in this environment is to structure labor relations so that the costs and the gains of increased productivity are equitably shared by the owners of the business enterprise and the workers in the firm. If this sense of equity is not achieved, the labor-management relationship is likely to degenerate into a situation of conflict, where mutual suspicion and distrust prevent the attainment of the cost and productivity objectives that, in the long run, are necessary for survival of the firm and the jobs it provides.

In his paper, Marshall argued that a more participative style of employee relations was needed to more closely involve workers in the decision making of a firm. One technique that has gained increasing attention by firms in the Southeast is quality circles or quality of worklife (QWL) programs. Raynor notes, however, that these attempts at participative management have often foundered for several reasons. One is that management does not have a major philosophical commitment to QWL programs and uses them only as short-term or stopgap measures in times of crisis; once the crisis is over, the firm reverts to business as usual. A second problem noted by Raynor is that in unionized firms the introduction of a QWL program is often perceived as a management ploy to weaken the union rather than a bona fide attempt at participative management.

The entire issue of unionism and collective bargaining in the Southeast in the 1980s was examined closely by our authors. As Marshall and Raynor observed, states in the Southeast have a much lower level of unionization than do many other states in the country. In Marshall's view, the low level of collective bargaining in the Southeast leaves low-wage workers without the bargaining power necessary to increase their level of earnings or to protect themselves from unilateral management decisions. Both he and Raynor argue, therefore, that collective bargaining is an indispensable component of industrial life that protects the interests of the worker. While they do not dispute the legal right to join unions, Robinson and Mack point out, however, that the low wage level in the Southeast has been a powerful magnet drawing new firms to the region. An issue that our authors draw attention to, therefore, is the difficult problem of increasing the wages and benefits of workers while at the same time preserving the competitive position of the business firm. The most obvious solution to this dilemma is renewed emphasis on increasing productivity, which—if accomplished—allows both goals to be met.

A final issue addressed by our authors is the prospects for conflict in the Southeast region between organized labor and management. Raynor is quite pessimistic about the prospects for cooperative labor relations. In his view, business has never accepted the obligation of collective bargaining nor the organizational legitimacy of unions as institutions. He argues that the mutual distrust engendered by the adversarial relationship is further exacerbated by the disruptive influence of management consultants and lawyers. The net result is that rather than being able to cooperate with management to improve the productivity of the firm, unions have to devote their energy to the struggle for survival. In his paper, Mack also foresees continued instability in labor relations. One key aspect of this, in his view, is the politicization of the labor law and its interpretation by the National Labor Relations Board. He also discusses the new techniques and approaches that the AFL-CIO hopes will result in new organizing victories in the Southeast and the tactics adopted by management to thwart these gains.